Teaching Students with

ADHD

Paula Galey

USER FRIENDLY RESOURCES

EDUCATIONAL PUBLISHERS
www.userfr.com

Book No. 599. Published by User Friendly Resources.

TITLE

Book Name: Teaching Students with ADHD
Book Code: 599
ISBN 13:   978-1-86968-477-8
Published: 2008

AUTHOR

Paula Galey

ACKNOWLEDGEMENTS

The publisher wishes to acknowledge the work of the following people:

Design: Cynthia Packman
Editor: Scanlan Communications

PUBLISHER

User Friendly Resources

United Kingdom Office	**New Zealand Office**	**Australian Office**
Premier House	PO Box 1820	PO Box 914
11 Marlborough Place	Christchurch	Mascot, NSW 2020
Brighton	Ph: 0508-500-393	Ph: 1800-553-890
East Sussex BN1 1UB	Fax: 0508-500-399	Fax: 1800-553-891
Ph: 0845-450-7502		
Fax: 0845-688-0199		

WEBSITE

www.userfr.com

E-MAIL

info@userfr.com

COPYING NOTICE

COPYRIGHT

User Friendly Resources specialises in publishing educational resources for teachers and students across a wide range of curriculum areas, at both primary and secondary levels. If you wish to know more about our resources, or if you think your resource ideas have publishing potential, please contact us at the above address.

Contents

Introduction 5

1. The Classroom Environment 13

Classroom Layout Plan 15
Classroom Layout Checklist 16

2. Completing Tasks 17

Sprint Sheet 21
On-task Self-monitoring Chart 22
Ribbon and Voucher 23
Phonics Chart 24
Personal Dictionary 25
Study Buddy System 26
Work Completion Checklist 30
Good Day's Work Sheet 31

3. Presenting Information 32

Model Work Sheets 33
Sample Lesson Outline 39
Learning Overview 40
Activity Ideas 42
Cooperative Learning Ideas 43
Role Cards 46
Peer-and Cross-age Tutoring Ideas 47

4. Teacher-Directed Teaching and Instructions 48

Instruction Comic Strip 49
Instruction Flash Cards 50

5. Organisation 52

Visual Timetable 54
Visual Timetable Pictures 55
List of Daily Supplies 56
Book Labels 57
Perpetual Calendar 58
Due Date Pictures 59
Routine Chart and Transition Red Card 60
Diary 61
Outstanding Organisation and Trophy of Tidiness 62
Picture Labels 63

6. Teacher Relationship 64

Teacher Interaction Tokens... 66
Hassle Log.. 67
Self-esteem Ideas.. 68

7. Parent Relationship 69

Individual Behaviour Plan.. 70
Individual Education Plan.. 71
Evaluation of Individual Behaviour Plan... 72
Home/ School Comments 73
Progress Reports and Positive Notes 74

8. Managing Behaviour 75

Behaviour Chart 79
Analysis of Antecedents and Consequences (ABC Sheet)................................. 80
Event Record 81
Goal Menu and Incentive Menu 82
Short-term Token Economy Contract 83
Results Graph for Week Ending 84
Response Cost Contract 85
Self-monitoring Rating Scale 86
Time Out System and Name Badge 87

9. Peer Relationships 88

Lessons to Support Respecting Individual Differences 90
Circle of Friends... 94
Social Behaviour Goals.. 95
Guided Playground Observation 96
Playground Plan 97

10. Teacher Intervention Plan. 98

Introduction

I've come to the frightening conclusion that I am the decisive element in the classroom. It is my personal approach that creates the climate. It is my daily mood that makes the weather. As a teacher I possess a tremendous power to make a child's life miserable or joyous. I can be a tool of torture or an instrument of inspiration. I can humiliate or heal. In all situations it is my response that decides whether a crisis will be escalated or de-escalated and a student humanised or dehumanised (Ginott, H. (1972) Teacher and Child, New York MacMillan p.34).

These words sum up the beliefs of teachers who advocate for applying an ecological model for students with special needs in schools. Achieving this model requires reconceptualising present paradigms of thought towards special education delivery, from one that focuses on the deficits of an individual student, to one that focuses on the organisational and instructional structures affecting the student. Such a paradigm shift would see schools embracing diversity and catering more effectively for all students. An ecological model supposes that all students are capable of being educated, that schools can make a difference in their students' lives, that diversity is valued, and that the impact of the teacher is viewed as significant. It alters the focus of interventions for students with special needs from prescribing therapy and changing individual personal characteristics to an analysis of the teaching and learning cycle. It embraces the concept of inclusion and contains a conviction that all students are equal members of the school, and that structures of organisation in a school should reflect provisions to enhance the learning of all students, including those with special needs.

This support book is based on an ecological model. It will assist teachers to accommodate for the special needs of students with Attention Deficit Hyperactivity Disorder (ADHD).

Accommodating their needs is achieved by adapting the classroom environment and enhancing teaching practices to anticipate the difficulties a student with ADHD will encounter, and so minimise the occurrence of inappropriate behaviours. This approach acknowledges the significance of the learning context and the efficacy of a teacher to generate relevant social contexts that will scaffold or facilitate a student's learning. It utilises practices of problem analysis which are founded on educational measures that examine the learning environment, the current teaching practices, the features of student behaviour, and the current levels of student's educational attainments. It takes into account the bearing that family, school, and community structures have on a student's performance. While ADHD is not curable, it can be made more manageable when a combination of medication, behavioural approaches and implementation of educational accommodations are used. In this way teachers can help "even the playing field" for students with ADHD.

Paula Galey

Students with ADHD at School

Although students with ADHD generally have normal or high IQ, they tend to underperform at school. Success at school requires students to have certain basic skills and characteristics. These include:

 **an ability to sustain attention** and exhibit impulse control so that they can focus on learning tasks

a healthy sense of self-esteem which contributes to a positive self-perception, willingness to persevere, and a positive attitude to learning in a safe and supportive environment

visual and auditory skills that allow them to take in information, discern its various parts, and memorise and perform symbolic concepts

thinking skills related to language and images so they can understand meanings, comprehend and apply previous knowledge, and organise, plan, and monitor tasks.

Although students with ADHD show considerable resilience and ingenuity just to keep their heads above water at school, these skills and characteristics are likely to challenge students and act as barriers to them accessing an education and optimising their potential.

Resource Structure

This book is divided into ten sections. These cover issues around attention and learning, organisation, impulsive behaviour and social behaviour. Each section outlines suggestions and materials that teachers can use to accommodate the needs of the student who has ADHD.

To tailor support to the needs of individuals, teachers can select and adapt material in the areas that students have difficulty with. It is also recommended that teachers use strategies that are effective for the whole class where feasible, rather than apply interventions on an individual level. This will ensure that support for students with ADHD is not too intrusive. It is important that teachers talk to students with ADHD and let them know that they are sincerely on their side or any interventions implemented will appear punitive and manipulative. Teachers who have students with ADHD in their classes can be advocates for them by helping others in the school to understand and accept the ADHD condition.

Check out what help is currently available for students with ADHD in this country. In conjunction with parents it may be worth investigating whether any financial support can be accessed to cover the expenses of any interventions that will assist the student at school.

The material in this book will be of benefit to:

- ◎ **Classroom teachers** who wish to better manage students in their class who have ADHD.

- ◎ **Specialist staff** who design interventions for students with learning or behaviour difficulties.

- ◎ **Teacher aides**, learning support staff, and special needs educators seeking to develop programmers to support particular students.

- ◎ **Parents** endeavouring to collaborate with the school to ensure the needs of their student are being effectively met.

- ◎ **Guidance staff** and teachers responsible for student management who wish to ensure all avenues of assistance for students are explored.

About ADHD

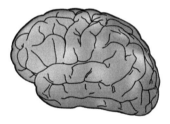

ADHD results from an immature or malfunctioning neurological system, caused by a neurochemical imbalance, that affects the way the part of the brain that regulates attention, activity levels, and impulsivity works.

Numerous studies suggest that the brain area affected is the frontal lobe, its connection with the basal ganglia and their relationship to central aspects of the cerebellum. Neuro-imaging research shows that there is less metabolic and electrical brain activity and less reactivity to stimulation in these regions in individuals with ADHD than in people in control groups. Additionally, blood evidence shows that students with ADHD may be deficient in fatty acids. These are not dietary-related but caused by an inability of the body to convert dietary essential fatty acids into the long chain EFA needed by the body for brain and eye function. People with ADHD often also experience physical symptoms like excessive thirst, perspiration, poor temperature sense control, ear troubles, eye troubles such as a squint, dark circles, puffiness, headaches, muscle or stomach pain, digestive upsets, food and drink cravings. They can also be infection prone, and have allergies.

ADHD is the most commonly diagnosed childhood mental condition, affecting approximately two to five per cent of school-age students, and indicative of a serious deficiency in a set of psychological abilities. ADHD is also thought to be identifiable in babies and toddlers who show symptoms of colic, cry a lot, are difficult to hold or cuddle, rock in their cots, bang their heads, are poor sleepers, have nappy rash, are fussy eaters, have unusual strength, climb, run away, and bite, hit or dominate others. The condition is diagnosed by a doctor or mental health expert. It is referenced as an early onset biological disorder characterised by a triad of symptoms including hyperactivity, inattention, and impulsivity. To meet the criteria for diagnosis these symptoms must begin before seven years of age, be inconsistent with developmental level, have been present for at least six months, be evident in two or more settings, and not due to any other psychological disorder.

Students with ADHD are a heterogeneous group and vary in the type, number, frequency and severity of their symptoms. The ADHD condition is divided into three sub-categories, however, ADHD is the technically correct term for all three types. The categories consist of ADHD combined type, ADHD predominantly inattentive, ADHD predominantly hyperactive or impulsive.

Inattention is characterised by:

- Failure to give attention to detail.
- Making careless mistakes in work.
- Avoiding tasks requiring sustained attention.
- Appearing not to listen when directly spoken to.
- Inability to follow through on instructions.
- Failure to finish work.
- Difficulty organising tasks.
- Difficulty sustaining attention.
- Losing things.
- Forgetfulness.
- Being easily distracted.

Hyperactivity is characterised by:

- Fidgeting and squirming.
- Inability to sit still.
- Running and climbing at inappropriate times.
- Difficulty playing quietly.
- Talking excessively.
- Acting as if driven.

Impulsive behaviour is characterised by:

- Blurting out answers before questions are finished.
- Inability to wait for turns.
- Interrupting and intruding on others.

Note: *these characteristics are indications only.*

ADHD is not the result of environmental factors. Family environment or parenting practices and peer relationships can exacerbate the symptoms of ADHD, but do not cause the condition. It is thought to have a genetic basis that is inherited. However some research indicates that not all students inherit the condition, but may develop ADHD symptoms from problems related to pregnancy, delivery, early childhood illness, head injury, trauma, or exposure to toxins. The condition affects three to four times more males than females and symptoms are generally noticeable at four to five years of age. Two thirds of clinically-referred students also often experience additional problems such as conduct disorder, anxiety problems, delayed motor development and learning problems, e.g. dyslexia, reading or spelling difficulties, language disorders or a significant weakness in maths. Indeed dyslexia, dyspraxia and ADHD are thought to be closely associated. It is projected that 50–75 per cent of students with ADHD will continue to live with the condition as adults, although levels of hyperactivity will decrease with age.

The effects of ADHD impact on all aspects of a student's life including their education, social relationships, family functioning, independence and self-sufficiency, occupational functioning, and the ability to adhere to social rules, norms and laws. The ADHD condition also has ramifications for the student's future, including a higher chance of dropping out from school and having few or no friends, the likelihood of engaging in anti-social acts or using illicit drugs and tobacco, a higher probability of teen pregnancy, a tendency to underperform at work, to speed excessively and have multiple car accidents, and the chance of being prone to adult depression or personality disorders.

ADHD is a poorly understood condition and people tend to have unrealistic expectations of the student which often leads to their condemnation and reprimand. This results in the emotional experience of ADHD being embarrassment, humiliation, self-castigation, and loss of confidence. This is particularly poignant given that most students with an illness are given comfort and assistance yet students with ADHD generally draw punishment and rejection.

A Multi-model Approach

A multi-model approach, tailored to the specific needs of each individual, is recommended for treating students with ADHD. This approach demands that medical, family, psychological, developmental, behavioural, social and educational factors are assessed to ensure a comprehensive, valid and reliable diagnosis. It requires healthcare professionals, educators and parents to work together to implement interventions. These might include a medical diagnosis which could entail a full check on eyesight, hearing, blood, thyroid function, worm or lice infestations, blood sugar levels, thrush, allergic reactions, chemical sensitivity and toxicity to ensure these are not contributing to the student's difficulties. It is likely that medical professionals will also wish to ensure that the student's nutrition is adequate for the growth and proper function of the developing brain and it may be recommended that artificial colours, flavours and antioxidant preservations are excluded from the diet.

Occupational therapy might be used to evaluate a student's functional ability in regards to gross and fine motor control, eye-hand coordination, visual / spatial relationships, body image and self concept. Further interventions may comprise parenting courses, behaviour therapy, remedial teaching, speech therapy and medication.

Medication

Generally the medication prescribed to students with ADHD is a stimulant. It is likely be named one of the following: Ritalin / Dexar (methylphenidate), Aurorix (moclobemide), Catapres (Clondine), Adderall, Adderall XR, Metadate CD, Concerta, Tofranil, Desipramine, Elavil, Tenex. Supplements of tuna oil high in docosahexaenoic acid combined with thyme oil may also help. Efalex is one such drug containing evening primrose oil, tuna oil, thyme oil and vitamin E which can be taken in conjunction with other medications. The purpose of medication is to improve the student's attention span, self control, behaviour control and social functioning.

Students with ADHD show diminished activity in the orbital frontal cortex region of the brain but medication alters dopamine production and improves the student's ability at self-regulation, planning, organising, and carrying out complex tasks. A doctor should closely monitor medication, but teachers also need to be aware of the student's medication as different medications produce different effects. For example some are quick-acting but short-lasting, whereas some take longer to work initially but have longer lasting effects. Being armed with this knowledge means that teachers can adapt their programme so that learning opportunities are optimally compatible with the effects of the student's medication. Furthermore the teacher can be an invaluable source for observing any side effects caused by the medication such as tics, seizures or involuntary movements which need to be reported immediately to the student's parents and subsequently a doctor.

Students with ADHD commonly have difficulty with some of the following:

- Handling frustration
- Being patient
- Being tolerant
- Complex problem solving
- Fine motor skills
- Managing anger
- Being rational
- Sustaining attention
- Persisting at and completing tasks
- Organisation
- Monitoring time
- Social acceptance
- Controlling their emotions and impulses
- Delaying their responses
- Listening
- Following instructions
- Transitioning to new activities
- Following through on instructions
- Concentrating
- Filtering out distractions and environmental noises
- Waiting their turn
- Judging consequences
- Self-monitoring
- Self-discipline
- Reading and interpreting social cues
- Physical coordination, e.g. being clumsy
- Peer relationships
- Managing anti-social behaviour
- Acting without thought or sense of safety
- Interrupting and intruding on others
- Excessive restlessness
- Constant motion
- Sitting still

- Understanding cause and effect
- Being able to verbalise rules but unable to translate these into behaviour
- Delaying gratification
- Learning from experience

They can also have:

- Poor short term memory
- Low self esteem
- Extremes of feelings
- Sensitivity to touch, pain and sound
- Activity levels – over active = hyperactive / under active = hypoactive

And:

- Unpredictable behaviour
- Need for constant supervision
- Be insatiable – never satisfied and can't let matters drop
- Ramble or say embarrassing things to others
- Interpret others as hostile
- Personalise others' actions

1 The Classroom Environment

 KEY IDEA: to tailor the classroom environment so that it will foster greater levels of attention and minimise impulsive behaviours.

Points to consider

- Open plan classrooms offer too many distractions, so avoid placing students with ADHD in these.

- Think carefully about where to seat students with ADHD. Seat them in desks, not at tables. Use a horseshoe layout or place the student between two studious classmates. Never seat the student beside other students who have challenging behaviour. Leave a decent distance between students' desks.

- Ideally, seat the student close to the front at either the extreme right or extreme left of the classroom. Ideally, seat the student close to either the extreme right or left of the classroom, especially if they are distracted by visual things. This limits their line of vision. However if the student is one who enjoys an audience or is more distracted by auditory things, seat them in the back row.

- Ensure the student is seated away from distractions such as windows or fishtanks and not near areas of high traffic or activity such as by the pencil sharpener or rubbish bin.

- Place the student near a blank wall or area of the classroom that is free from engaging displays so the surroundings adjacent to the student are as uninteresting as possible. This will make schoolwork the more interesting option.

- Consider making a study carrel by cutting a box in half-length ways and removing the top and bottom. Allow the student to decorate it. Use pegs on it to attach their worksheets.

- Acknowledge that the student with ADHD will have difficulty staying seated. Avoid confrontation on this issue by allowing the student to move around the room. Limit their territory by indicating the perimeter of movement allowed. Consider allowing the student an opportunity for whole body movement by letting them stand at their desk or spread out on the floor to work, from time to time.

- Provide regular breaks for physical activity and physical movement. These might include stretch breaks, trips to the office, taking notes to other teachers, feeding the class pet, etc.

- Use background music to minimise distractions or have a recording of the ocean, which will offer a sense of calmness. Baroque music has been found to enhance the brain's processing capacity. Alternatively permit the student to wear ear muffs, ear plugs or stereo headsets playing white noise or music to filter out environmental distractions.

The Classroom Environment

- Some believe that people think better if the thinking is accompanied by mouth movement as this integrates the thinking process with the nervous system. It may be beneficial to review no eating or chewing policies in classrooms.

- As students with ADHD are often sensitive to light, ensure the room has low-intensity lighting. Alternatively, let the student shade their eyes by wearing a baseball cap.

- Ensure the classroom ventilation is adequate.

- As students with ADHD have difficulty regulating hot and cold, remind them to adjust their clothing to adapt to the temperature.

Implementation Steps

1. Use the **Classroom Layout Plan** to help you make decisions about where best to seat the student and to ensure the classroom environment fosters effective learning.

2. Tick the **Classroom Layout Checklist** to affirm that you have considered all the main points.

3. On the plan, draw in the key features of your classroom including rubbish bins, pencil sharpeners, wall displays, windows etc.

4. Initially use the map as a behavioural tool by observing the student to see where the trouble spots are so that you can arrange the environment accordingly. Some key questions to ask yourself include: What are the problem behaviours? What should the student be doing instead? When and where do the problem behaviours occur? How does the class react? When and where is the student usually on-task?

5. Once you have collected this data, pencil in where you consider the ideal place is to situate the student's desk, then assess the effectiveness of this in relation to the distractions listed. Remember, attention also needs to be given to the students who will be seated near the student with ADHD.

6. If you have decided a study carrel will be beneficial, gather the necessary resources and construct it.

7. Decide how much freedom of movement you will permit the student around their desk area and indicate this on the layout plan.

8. Once you are satisfied with the location you have selected, physically rearrange the desks and indicate to the student the area they can move within.

9. Assess the lighting, ventilation and temperature in your room and adjust accordingly. Keep a thermometer permanently in your room. Assign a student to monitor it and alert their peers when they may need to regulate their clothing or access better ventilation.

10. Consider how you will manage physical activity breaks. For example, whether you will involve the whole class or provide errand opportunities for the student with ADHD and write these into the space provided on the classroom layout plan.

11. Experiment with music and sounds. Write on the plan which times of the day's schedule these are suitable. Organise the equipment you need for this.

12. Decide what your policy will be regarding eating in class and indicate this on the plan.

Classroom Layout Plan

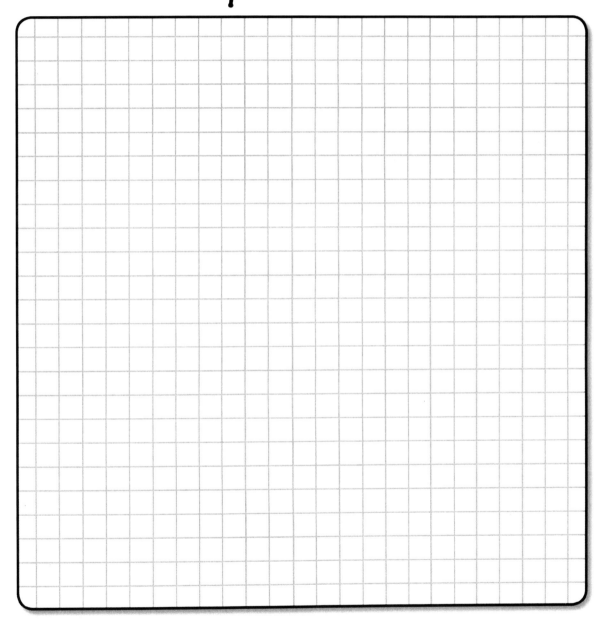

Notes :

Classroom Layout Checklist

☐ Seating position and layout
☐ Peers the student is seated beside
☐ Minimised distractions
☐ Study carrel
☐ Movement territory
☐ Physical activity
☐ Music / sound
☐ Eating policy
☐ Lighting
☐ Ventilation
☐ Temperature

② Completing Tasks

 KEY IDEA: to implement strategies that optimise the student's ability to complete tasks when working independently.

Points to consider

- Use teacher-directed lessons rather than independent work when teaching students with ADHD. However, do try to provide some opportunity for self-paced work.

- Avoid work that requires copying in timed situations. Instead issue carbon paper and have a peer write the notes on the student's behalf. You could also have someone type the notes into the class computer and print them off.

- Only give assignments one at a time to avoid the student feeling overloaded, as this will decrease the likelihood of the student completing any task.

- Chunk lengthy assignments into smaller segments in collaboration with the student. Talk through the tasks and the sequence in which they are best completed. Give short time limits to complete each task and enforce these consistently.

- If the student has a learning difficulty in a particular area, like Maths, consider letting them answer every second problem instead of each one.

- Set accuracy goals in addition to speed and social behaviour goals. This will address the tendency that students with ADHD may have to rush through their work without caring about its quality.

- Students with ADHD often have a very poor concept of time. However they can thrive on challenges. Use an hourglass, stopwatch or cooking timer to help with this, set the timer and say, "You have five minutes to complete this exercise. If you finish in that time that's great, if not the consequence will be…" Or for younger students set the timer and say, " You have four minutes to complete this task, when the timer beeps you must show me what you have done." Alternatively use the timer as something to race against, "How long do you think it will take to do these four questions? Let's see if you can do it."

- Use an audio-cue such as a tape with tones recorded at irregular intervals to teach students to self-monitor their on-task behaviour. Or simply do this by dropping a counter on the student's desk at certain intervals as a cue to monitor whether they are on-task.

- Encourage on-task behaviour by monitoring the student closely at least three times during each lesson.

- Students with ADHD often have trouble spelling and commonly ask, "What's that word?" or, "How do you spell…?" Consider using a phonetic approach to assist these students and issuing them with a personalised dictionary. Allow the student to move their finger or pencil across the page when reading and to place fingers between words for spacing when writing. Provide graph paper in Maths to help the student to organise numbers and columns.

- Students with ADHD are often verbally expressive but can have difficulty putting their ideas on paper. Allow them to do work by dictation or to use a word processor, as this will yield better results since writing is taken out of the equation. Also ensure you teach writing skills, for example how to structure sentences and paragraphs.

- Instigate a "study buddy" system in which classmates who have a cooperative and understanding attitude volunteer to assist the student by helping them with work-related problems. Establish rules for this system and ensure both students are aware of what types of assistance are appropriate. Never recruit students to be study buddies, use only volunteers and rotate the study buddies regularly.

- Provide model examples of setting-out formats that are regularly used and other examples of any work set.

- Teach the student to check that their work is finished before handing it in. Use a checklist that outlines the steps that must be completed before something can be considered finished e.g. draft written, proof-read, partner proof-read, corrected, shown to the teacher, published.

- Have a system for keeping track of task completion. This can be achieved in a variety of ways. For example, for work to be published put the students' names on cards on the wall. When it's finished attach it to the wall above the name card. Each week make a checklist of all the students' names and class activities and tick each item off as it is completed. Alternatively allocate each student an ID number that corresponds to the alphabetical roll. When students hand in their work put it in ID number order and use as a quick way to check who has not completed a task.

- Encourage students to develop personal strategies such creating a visual picture they can use as a checklist so they learn to take responsibility for ensuring they complete all tasks set each day.

- Issue vouchers for work completion which can be a way of earning an incentive.

Implementation Steps

1. Evaluate your teaching programme each term to check that the ratio of independent and teacher-directed assignments is balanced.

2. Make adaptations to assignment requirements to accommodate for learning difficulties and to increase the student's chances of success at completing the task.

3. When you issue students with an independent assignment use the **Sprint Sheet** to chunk the assignment into manageable parts. Enlarge the sheet to A3 size if necessary. In conjunction with the student write in the instructions for each step inside each part of the race track and set the speed, accuracy and social goals. Have the student evaluate their success at meeting their goals at each step by colouring in the relevant medal.

4. Organise a timer and show the student how to use it.

5. Provide the student with the **On-task Self-monitoring Chart** and ask them to colour the appropriate face to show whether they were on-task when the audio cue or counter was given. Consider issuing the **On-task Ribbon** or **Voucher** as an incentive if the student manages to be on-task for a predetermined number of cues.

6. Encourage on-task behaviour by monitoring the student at the start of the lesson then redirecting them and checking their understanding about a quarter of the way through the lesson. Increase encouragement three-quarters of the way through the lesson to maintain their on-task behaviour.

7. Give the student an enlarged copy of the **Phonics Chart** to assist them with sounding out words and a copy of the **Personal Dictionary** to record words they commonly have difficulty spelling. Have the student paste these into their book or attach them to their desk. Encourage the student to spell the word themselves using the phonics sheet as a guide. Have it checked by you or a study buddy before writing it in the appropriate place on the personal dictionary. It may be useful to give the student a blank laminated piece of A4 white paper that they can write in their attempts using non-permanent pens. If they spell the word correctly there is no need to record it in their personal dictionary, as it is one that they already know. If the student misspells the word by only one or two incorrect letters bring the student's visual focus to those letters by changing the letter size or colour when they write it in their personal dictionary e.g. horce would be written as hor**S**e.

8. Decide whether you will let the student use alternatives to hand writing to record their ideas and organise the necessary equipment. It is important to consider what skill you actually want the student to master when making this decision.

9. Establish the **Study Buddy System** by choosing appropriate students. See page 93 in the *Peer Relationships* section of this resource for ideas on how this can be suitably introduced to peers. Complete the **Study Buddy Roster** to show which students are acting in this role and when. When students have had a turn they colour in their name so you can easily see who is next in line to act as a study buddy. Allocate some time to define the role and train students using the **Study Buddy Job Description**. During this time establish and record the rules that will apply in your particular classroom

for study buddy tasks. This might include that students are allowed to talk openly but quietly about the work, but are not permitted to pester or socialise with their study buddy. They can ask questions such as, "Do these words need to be in sentences?" but not questions such as, "What's the answer to this?" For work you consider suited to a study buddy complete the **Teacher Instruction Activity Card** indicating the type of teaching expected by drawing on ideas listed on the job description. Use the **Study Buddy Evaluation Chart** to assist you to monitor the system and provide the study buddy feedback. Discuss the experience with the study buddy immediately after they have finished acting in the role and recording a brief comment. At the end of each term issue the study buddies with the **Study Buddy Certificate** to acknowledge their efforts.

10. Create and display posters in the classroom with model examples of setting-out formats. Remember to demonstrate any work set with a teacher example, if possible.

11. Before accepting work issue the student with the **Work Completion Checklist** which indicates what they should have done for the task to be completely finished. Have them check through this before submitting their work for marking.

12. When the student has completed the work give them a voucher. Students who earn a certain number then redeem it for an incentive. Vouchers can also be used on a whole class basis. Drawing one out at the end of the week earns a prize.

13. Check the student's name off using your preferred checklist system.

14. Issue the student with the **Good Day's Work** picture each morning and write in each balloon the tasks to be finished by the end of the day. The student colours in each balloon as they complete their work.

Sprint Sheet

Project Name _____

Key:
Gold
Silver
Bronze

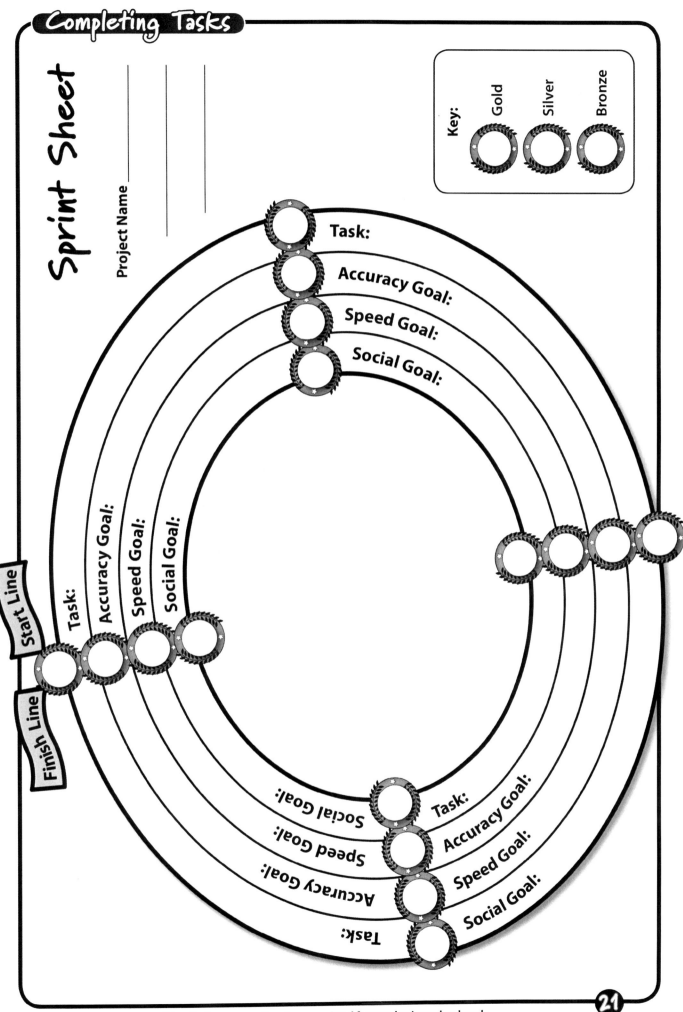

Task:

Accuracy Goal:

Speed Goal:

Social Goal:

Start Line

Finish Line

Task:

Accuracy Goal:

Speed Goal:

Social Goal:

Task:

Accuracy Goal:

Speed Goal:

Social Goal:

On-task Self-monitoring Chart

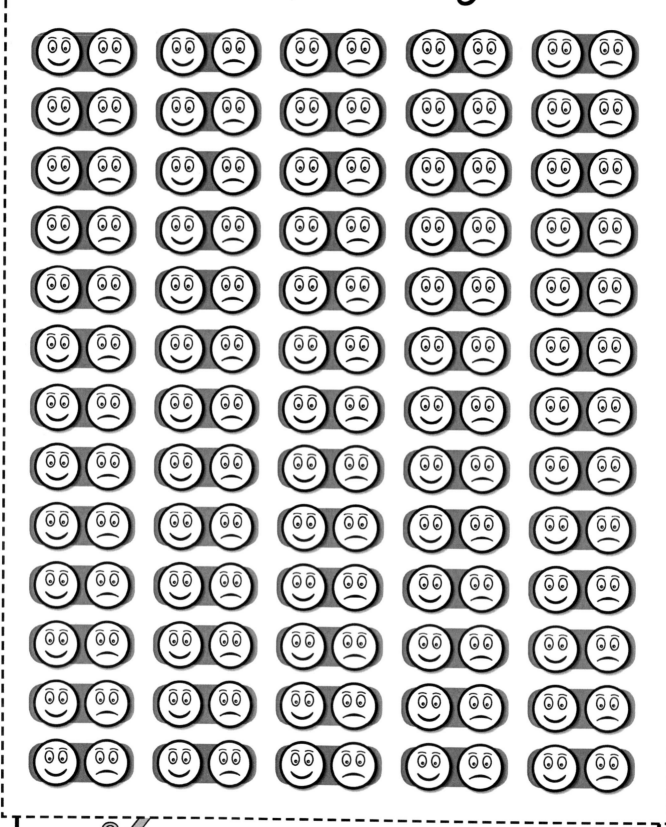

Ribbon

This ribbon is awarded to

_____

for being on-task ____% of the time.

_____
Teacher's Signature

Voucher

This medal of work management is awarded to

_____

for completing

_____

_____

_____
Teacher's Signature   *Date*

Phonics Chart

Bl b<u>lue</u>	Cl <u>cl</u>own	Fl <u>fl</u>ower	Gl <u>gl</u>asses	Pl <u>pl</u>ate	Sl <u>sl</u>ide	Br <u>br</u>oom	Cr <u>cr</u>own	Dr <u>dr</u>agon
Fr <u>fr</u>og	Gr <u>gr</u>apes	Pr <u>pr</u>am	Tr <u>tr</u>actor	Tw <u>tw</u>ins	Sc <u>sc</u>arecrow	Sk <u>sk</u>ateboard	Sm <u>sm</u>oke	Sn <u>sn</u>ow
Sp <u>sp</u>ider	St <u>st</u>amp	Sw <u>sw</u>ing	Wh <u>wh</u>ale	Ch <u>ch</u>air	Sh <u>sh</u>ark	Th <u>th</u>umb	Ph <u>ph</u>one	Qu <u>qu</u>een
Kn <u>kn</u>ight	Wr <u>wr</u>ap	Un <u>un</u>cle	C <u>c</u>at	E k<u>e</u>y <u>e</u>gg and b<u>ee</u>	G <u>g</u>oat and <u>g</u>iraffe	I k<u>i</u>te and <u>i</u>gloo	U <u>u</u>mbrella and <u>u</u>nicorn	Dge e<u>dge</u>
Tch wi<u>tch</u>	Nk ta<u>nk</u>	Ir s<u>ir</u>	Or protract<u>or</u>	Air f<u>air</u> ground	Are bus f<u>are</u>	Eer ch<u>eer</u>	Ear <u>ear</u>ring	Err <u>err</u>and
War a<u>war</u>d	Wor <u>Wor</u>n	En eat<u>en</u>	On butt<u>on</u>	Age Dam<u>age</u>	Ly slow<u>ly</u>	Zle puz<u>zle</u>	Kle twin<u>kle</u>	Ous jeal<u>ous</u>
Ple ap<u>ple</u>	Gle Jun<u>gle</u>	Dle daw<u>dle</u>	Cle mus<u>cle</u>	Ous m<u>ouse</u>	Ble mum<u>ble</u>	Ice m<u>ice</u>	Ed shout<u>ed</u>	Ess princ<u>ess</u>
Oi n<u>oi</u>se	Oy b<u>oy</u>	Ew f<u>ew</u>	Tion atten<u>tion</u>	Sion ten<u>sion</u>	Cial spe<u>cial</u>	Re <u>re</u>member	Oo m<u>oo</u>n	Oo b<u>oo</u>k
Oa c<u>oa</u>t	X <u>x</u>ylophone box	Ea l<u>ea</u>f	a-e g<u>a</u>t<u>e</u>	i-e b<u>i</u>k<u>e</u>	o-e music n<u>o</u>t<u>e</u>s	u-e c<u>u</u>b<u>e</u>	Amp l<u>amp</u>	Que uni<u>que</u>
Ide r<u>ide</u>	O oct<u>o</u>pus	Ot c<u>ot</u>	Op m<u>op</u>	Ack s<u>ack</u>	Eck n<u>eck</u>	Sl <u>sl</u>ide	Str <u>str</u>ing	Silent w <u>w</u>rap
Silent b lam<u>b</u>	Scr <u>scr</u>aps	Au s<u>au</u>cer	Ch (k) mi<u>ch</u>ael	Ible sens<u>ible</u>	Igh n<u>igh</u>t	Ince m<u>ince</u>	Ance d<u>ance</u>	Eigh sl<u>eigh</u>
Geon sur<u>geon</u>	Ology bi<u>ology</u>	Omy astron<u>omy</u>	Ped <u>ped</u>estrian	Peo <u>peo</u>ple	Phe apostro<u>phe</u>	Psy <u>psy</u>chology	Ee w<u>ee</u>k	Ch <u>ch</u>urch
Ur f<u>ur</u>	Ie p<u>ie</u>	Eign for<u>eign</u>	Gue ton<u>gue</u>	Augh l<u>augh</u>	Athy symp<u>athy</u>	Aphy biogr<u>aphy</u>	Gu <u>gu</u>ide	Eous gorg<u>eous</u>
Ence experi<u>ence</u>	Cious deli<u>cious</u>	Ue c<u>ue</u>	Ou s<u>ou</u>r	Gh enou<u>gh</u>	Et turr<u>et</u>	Ure dent<u>ure</u>	Ough r<u>ough</u>	Able t<u>able</u>
Ei h<u>ei</u>ght	Ity c<u>ity</u>	Ck clo<u>ck</u>	Ay d<u>ay</u>	Aw p<u>aw</u>	Ow c<u>ow</u>	Ar st<u>ar</u>	Ai sn<u>ai</u>l	Ur ch<u>ur</u>ch
Ing <u>ring</u>	Ong str<u>ong</u>	A <u>a</u>pple and <u>a</u>pron						

Personal Dictionary

Aa	_____	Nn	_____
Bb	_____	Oo	_____
Cc	_____	Pp	_____
Dd	_____	Qq	_____
Ee	_____	Rr	_____
Ff	_____	Ss	_____
Gg	_____	Tt	_____
Hh	_____	Uu	_____
Ii	_____	Vv	_____
Jj	_____	Ww	_____
Kk	_____	Xx	_____
Ll	_____	Yy	_____
Mm	_____	Zz	_____

Study Buddy System

Study Buddy Roster

Colour in your name after you have had a turn as a study buddy for: _____

Date:	Date:	Date:	Date:
Who: _____ When:	Who: _____ When:	Who: _____ When:	Who: _____ When:
Who: _____ When:	Who: _____ When:	Who: _____ When:	Who: _____ When:
Who: _____ When:	Who: _____ When:	Who: _____ When:	Who: _____ When:
Who: _____ When:	Who: _____ When:	Who: _____ When:	Who: _____ When:
Who: _____ When:	Who: _____ When:	Who: _____ When:	Who: _____ When:
Who: _____ When:	Who: _____ When:	Who: _____ When:	Who: _____ When:
Who: _____ When:	Who: _____ When:	Who: _____ When:	Who: _____ When:

26

Study Buddy Job Description

Study buddy qualities

To be a good study buddy you need to:

- be friendly
- be positive
- be encouraging
- be patient
- be able to give feedback
- listen and ask good questions
- suggest and coach
- help your buddy without doing the work for them
- find ways to help your buddy remember things
- be able to judge how well your time as study buddy was spent.

Study buddy responsibilities

As a study buddy you may need to:

- answer your buddy's questions
- show your buddy how to do something
- test your buddy to see if they can do something and if not, teach them how before testing them again
- take turns by doing the first task then letting your buddy take a turn and so on
- do the task together
- show your buddy what they have done correctly and then point out what they still need to do or where they have made an error
- show your buddy how to do a task by using easier words or by showing them a drawing or diagram
- give your buddy an example
- model the task for your buddy
- give your buddy clues or hints
- relate the task to something else your buddy has already done
- pause to let your buddy try to do the task alone, prompt your buddy by giving them a clue, then praise them when they get the task right.

Study buddy rules in this class

- _____
- _____
- _____
- _____

Completing Tasks

Teacher Instruction Activity Card

Curriculum Area _____

Topic _____

Aim _____

Type of Teaching _____

Activity _____

Study Buddy Evaluation Chart

Date/Study Buddy	Task	Study Buddy Comment	Teacher Comment

Study Buddy Certificate

Study Buddy Certificate

This certificate is awarded to

_____

**In acknowledgement of your efforts
as a classroom study buddy.**

_____
Signed

Study Buddy Certificate

This certificate is awarded to

_____

**In acknowledgement of your efforts
as a classroom study buddy.**

_____
Signed

Work Completion Checklist For:

_____

✓ Before I hand in this work I need to check these things have been done

☐ _____

☐ _____

☐ _____

☐ _____

☐ _____

☐ _____

☐ _____

☐ _____

☐ _____

☐ _____

☐ _____

If you can complete these tasks, you will have done...

...A Good Day's Work!

③ Presenting Information

 KEY IDEA: to present information in a way that will capture and sustain the student's attention and assist them to master new learning.

Points to consider: Worksheets

- Reduce the amount of work presented on each worksheet to avoid overwhelming the student. Ideally only one to two activities should be on each page and white space should predominate. Alternatively, if you are using prepared worksheets with numerous activities on them, cut the worksheet up and give the student one piece at a time.

- Use off-white or buff-coloured paper to reduce glare and large dark black print. Where possible avoid hand-written worksheets.

- Keep the format simple. Don't have unrelated illustrations on the page, as these are visually distracting. Introduce novelty and use highly motivating materials such as a range of diverse shapes or textures.

- Underline or highlight key directions, main points and new vocabulary in different colours or draw borders around the parts you want emphasised. Also encourage the student to use coloured pencils to highlight items of significance.

- Keep instructions simple. Where feasible present information and instructions in the form of flowcharts or mind maps.

Implementation Steps

1. Design your own or scan the **Model Worksheets, Mindmaps and Flowcharts** into your computer and enter the work you want the student to attempt. Remember to keep the language as simple as possible. Select the mindmaps and flow charts that are appropriate for the information you are presenting. These provide a visual representation for how a student can view the relationship between ideas, concepts or meanings. They are hierarchical, going from general to specific and use verbs to link ideas. They serve as an aid to constructing knowledge and clarifying relationships and are useful tools for teaching and learning.

2. Use the computer functions to highlight or border important features.

3. Ask the person who orders the office supplies to purchase off-white or buff coloured paper and use this for printing.

4. If you are designing your own worksheets occasionally glue on a piece of fabric as a page border or cut the paper using jagged scissors or present the sheet in a different shape, e.g. a heart for novelty value.

Model Work Sheets

Brainstorm Web

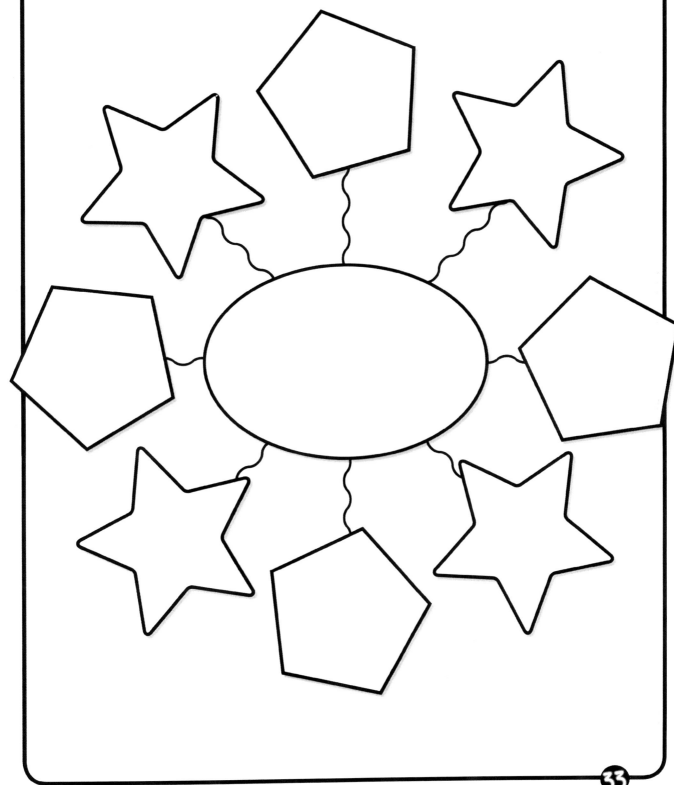

Flow Chart

Main Ideas and Supporting Details

Main Heading

Details

Example

Points to consider : Assessments

- When testing avoid long assessments. Use short quizzes regularly instead. If mastery can be observed in 20 questions, don't set 40.

- Try to provide practice assessments.

- Isolate the student during assessments to minimise distractions.

- Monitor assessments to ensure the student is following instructions accurately.

- If the student has difficulty with written language try adapting the assessment by using either a multi-choice format or an oral exam. The student could also tape record answers or draw pictures. You could also read the assessment aloud to the student, or enable them to apply their learning in a real-life setting. Try shortening the length or extending the time frame of the assessment, if it seems appropriate.

Implementation Steps

1. Give the student a practice assessment to do at home the night before an assessment so they are familiar with the format.

2. Where feasible, alter the format of written assessments using one of the ideas mentioned in the *Points to Consider* section.

3. If practicable arrange for the student to complete the assessment in a private room where they will not be distracted or able to distract others. If this is not possible consider using a study carrel to provide privacy.

4. If the assessment is a long one, organise for the student to complete it over several days rather than in one sitting or reduce the number of questions the student is required to answer.

5. Monitor the student closely during the initial part of the assessment to ensure they have understood what is expected.

Points to consider: Teaching Strategies

- Students with ADHD can get progressively worse at remaining on-task over the course of the day. **So set up formal learning opportunities in the morning** and other activities in the afternoon. The optimal period for attention after students have taken their medication differs between medications. Discuss this with the parents and use the medication window to schedule the most attention-demanding tasks.

- **Highlight main points** in a lesson by using different coloured whiteboard markers to emphasise key points and new vocabulary. Provide a lesson outline with key concepts and vocabulary to the student the night prior to teaching any new content.

- Keep lessons brief or **chunk** longer presentations into small segments. Try to **vary the pace** of the lesson and the level of your speech.

- Students with ADHD are visually-oriented, so use **graphic facilitation techniques** when presenting information. This technique synthesises ideas into visual models to help make abstract ideas concrete and serves as a powerful mnemonic to refresh memories. Also encourage the student to develop mental images of key concepts and ensure you ask them to describe their visualisations.

- If presenting written material use a **preview strategy.** Here you only expose the part of the page to students that is relevant at the time.

- Use **multi-model presentations** of lesson content. For example, incorporate hands-on activities, 3D models or role-play, learning stations or game-like activities to teach concepts. Computer-assisted learning is visually stimulating and offers tactile and kinaesthetic involvement.

- When students work in groups **allocate roles** to each individual so that all group members have a valuable part to play and are responsible for specific contributions.

- Use **cooperative learning** activities in small groups, particularly those that require the student to contribute to the group by fulfilling a particular role or supplying a specific piece of information. When students work cooperatively in groups and assist one another to accomplish learning tasks, learning can be enhanced. Students also develop interpersonal skills and skills in problem solving and complex thinking and experience gains in self esteem. Additionally, cooperative learning improves the classroom climate as students are more likely to be actively involved, self-directed in their learning, develop communication skills and become more accepting and supportive of their peers. Students learn to value individual differences and respect diversity by understanding how all members can contribute to each other's achievements. This method of teaching is of particular benefit to students with learning and behavioural difficulties, as it helps to facilitate social and emotional development and foster relationships.

- Use **peer tutoring** or cross-age tutoring. Here the teacher facilitates learning through structuring activities that require students of different ability levels to work collaboratively in pairs. This strategy utilises the natural support relationships that spontaneously exist amongst students and provides an opportunity for them to acquire cooperative skills while mastering content. The basic principles of peer tutoring are founded in the notion of **scaffolding**. Those students, who act as tutors in peer tutoring programmes also make significant learning improvement, experience growth in self-concept and develop a sense of individual responsibility. Teachers find that establishing peer tutoring programmes provides more effective use of time and greater flexibility to facilitate students' learning on an individual basis.

Implementation Steps

1. Evaluate your class schedule to work out whether lessons that require the greatest amounts of attention are scheduled for mornings.

2. Speak to the students' parents to plan when is the best time for taking advantage of the medication window.

3. Minimise environmental distractions by sticking to your seating plan.

4. Ensure periods of teacher-directed discussion are kept brief and if necessary break up the time the student is required to listen by interspersing with activities.

5. Provide the student with a completed copy of the **Sample Lesson Outline**, or write it up on your whiteboard prior to teaching. If possible, issue this to the student the night before so they have time to familiarise themselves with new concepts. In the lesson target section of the lesson outline fill in the objectives you want the student to have mastered by the end of the lesson. Ensure you refer the student to these regularly so they know what is expected, and can use them to reflect on their progress and success. In the title section write in the title of your lesson. In the key question section write in a big picture / overview question regarding the content of the lesson to focus the student on the lesson's intentions. The start task is designed for a 5 to 10 minute activity that links this lesson to a previous lesson. The activity box is where you record the main activities of the lesson and any related diagrams. The keyword space is for the lesson's specific keywords. Write these in capital letters so they stand out and ask the student to provide a definition of these at the conclusion of the lesson. Try and colour coordinate the various sections, e.g. targets in red, key question in black, start task in green, activities in blue, and key words in orange, and use the same colours with consistency each time you complete the lesson outline. Highlight or underline things that you consider important so the eye is drawn towards them, which will increase the likelihood the student will process the information.

6. Ask the student to complete the **Learning Overview** at the end of the teaching period to evaluate what they have learnt. The heading / keyword template is used by asking the student to cut each one into cards and then sort the keywords under the appropriate headings before organising them into the grid. Alternatively use one of the mindmap or flowchart ideas provided in the worksheet section following. Enlarge if necessary.

7. Try to use **graphic facilitation** techniques when you record information in a lesson and encourage the student to use these in their own records of the lesson. Graphic facilitation basically requires you to draw a picture to represent ideas. Only very simplistic drawings are required.

8. Use the **Activity Ideas** lists supplied to assist you with methods of teaching that will be particularly motivating to the student. You might choose to use the ideas as a way of presenting information to the student, or as an activity for the student to complete to help them process the learning.

9. Where possible use the **Cooperative Learning Ideas** supplied. These ideas provide a basis for organising student interactions. Each activity can be used where relevant and associated to a particular learning outcome decided by the teaching needs. By combining a few of these activities and modifying them to suit the lesson objectives, teachers can create interesting interactive lessons. A wealth of these and other cooperative learning ideas can be found in books by Spencer Kagan.

10. When asking the students to work in groups, allocate the **Role Cards** to help ensure individual accountability and assist with organisation. Photocopy each onto different coloured card and laminate.

11. Use the **Peer-or Cross-tutoring** style of teaching in at least one curriculum area each term. Use the steps listed on the associated resource to assist you to choose a curriculum area and implement the programme.

Sample Lesson Outline

Lesson Objectives	Title	Instructions for activities, diagrams, etc	Activities
	Key Question		
	Start Task		
	Keywords		

Learning Overview

Headings

Main Ideas

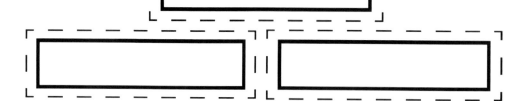

Keywords

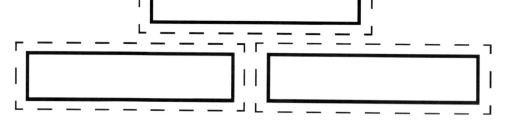

What I Learned

Name : _____

Learning Overview

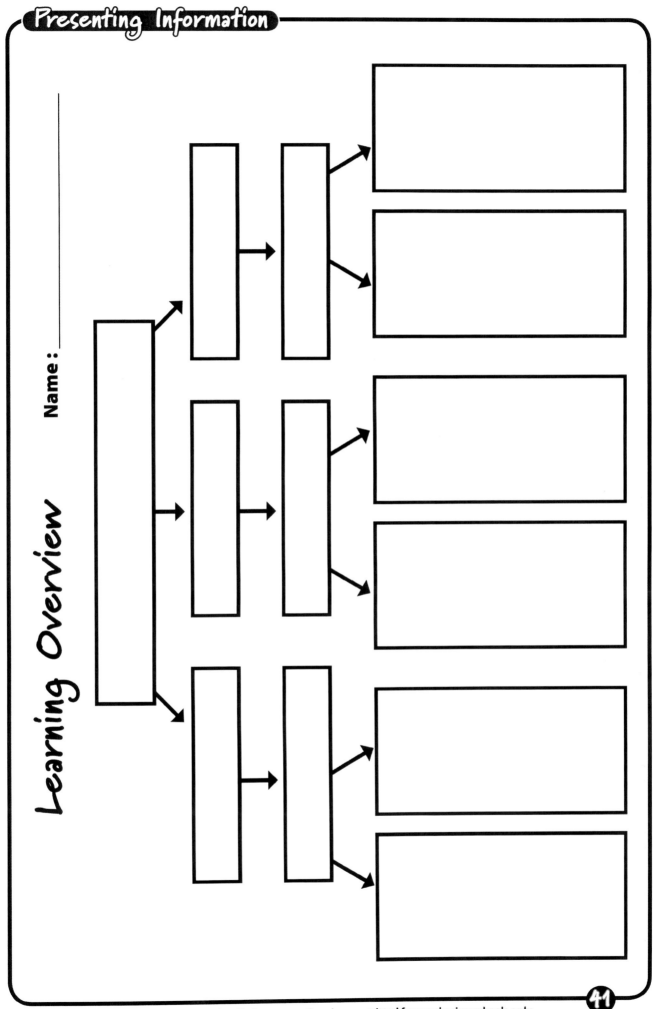

Activity Ideas

3D room displays
Acting/ dramatisation
Advertisements
Art activities
Audio-taping
Board games
Cartooning
Charts
Collages
Collecting
Comic strips
Composing
Computer games
Constructing
Dancing
Demonstrations
Diagramming
Dioramas
Dramatisations
Drawing
Experiments
Exploring
Field studies
Fieldtrips
Flashcards
Flow-charting
Games
Graphing
Illustrating with paints, markers, chalk, crayons, charcoal, clay
Interviews
Inventions
Investigations

Lab work
Learning centres
Make overhead transparencies
Maps
Mobiles
Models
Mosaics
Murals
Observing
Painting
Pantomiming
Performing
Photographs
Photos
Plays
Poems
Posters
Puppet making
Puzzle making
Puzzles
Radio broadcasts
Role play
Sculpting
Singing
Sports
Statues
Story boarding
Symbols
Timelines
Videos/films
Videotapes
Whiteboard

Cooperative Learning Ideas

Match Mine: *this activity is ideal for vocabulary building.* Give students a grid and lesson-related pictures on cards. One student arranges the pictures on their grid then must give clues to the other student using only oral communication. The other student must attempt to arrange them in the same way on their grid.

Numbered Heads Together: *use this activity to review mastery of a lesson.* Organise the students into groups of four. Ask the groups a question and then provide time for the group to consult to make sure everyone knows the answer. The teacher then asks one student randomly from the group to provide the answer.

Colour Coded Cards: *use this activity to help students memorise facts.* The students test one another using flash cards to memorise the facts but acquire points only for improvement in each round.

Pairs Check: *this activity is designed to help students practise skills.* Students work in pairs within a group of four. Each pair works together to solve a problem and then after every two problems, checks with the other pair to see if they have arrived at the same answer.

Three Step Interview: *use this activity for developing concept knowledge e.g. hypothesis development, thoughts pertaining to a story, knowledge acquired from a lesson, etc.* Students take turns to interview one another in pairs then share the information they gained from the interview with another pair.

Think Pair Share: *this activity can be applied to generate prior knowledge on a topic or to review learning.* Students work individually to brainstorm their ideas, then pair up with another student to discuss them. They join together with another group to create a collaborative brainstorm of all their ideas.

Team Word Webbing: *this activity can be applied to learning involving multiple relationships between concepts.* Students work in groups of three. They write simultaneously on a sheet of paper to draw a mind map showing main concepts, supporting elements and bridges to represent the relationships between ideas and concepts.

Simultaneous Round Table: *this activity is useful for extracting prior knowledge or recalling information, and can also be used for proofreading work.* In groups of four, students are given four separate pieces of paper with different headings on them. Each student writes one answer on each piece of paper then passes it on to the next group member who writes a new piece of information on it before passing it on. In the case of proof reading, each member looks to make one correction or each student may have a task, e.g. one checks spelling and another for punctuation.

Inside Outside Circle: *use this activity to review or process information.*
Students stand in pairs in two concentric circles. The people in the inside circle
face out and those in the outside circle face in. The teacher poses a question that the
students answer by telling their circle partner. The teacher then calls a certain number of
rotations and the outside circle moves this many rotations to link up with a new partner.

Partners: *this activity can be used to master or create new content.* Students work in pairs on
a topic. Then each person in the pair partners up with another person from another pair
and shares their information before returning to the original pair with the new information
they have got.

Jigsaw: *this activity can be applied to acquiring or*
reviewing new content. Students are assigned to small
groups. Each student in that group works with members
of other groups who have been assigned a corresponding
topic. Once they have become an 'expert' at that topic
they return to their original group where they teach that
topic to the others. All students in the group are assessed
on all four topics covered. It is possible to present their
project in a jigsaw format, with each member's information
presented on one piece of the jigsaw and then the whole
group's work fitting together to form a completed jigsaw.

Human Treasure Hunt: *this activity can be*
used to learn new information or review learnt
information. Provide each student in the
class with a sheet containing topic-related
questions. Supply the resources necessary for
the students to answer these questions and
give them a brief time span in which to do so.
At the end of the time limit ask the students to
walk around the room and trade answers with
their classmates in an attempt to answer all
the questions on the sheet. Each student can
only acquire one answer from any other student.

Rally Table: *this activity is useful for brainstorming.* One student reads their ideas to another
student who ticks off similar ideas they have had and adds any new ideas to their list. The
process is then reversed and repeated with another pair of classmates so that a group ends
up with one list of accumulated thoughts.

Hide and Seek: *this activity is helpful for reviewing material.* Attach stickers to students'
backs with titles of your topic written on them. Students wander around the room asking
questions about the topic to which their classmates can only answer yes or no. Students
use these responses to try and figure out what is written on the sticker.

Crossword Chaos: *this is a suitable activity for sharing information with others so students can learn from each other.* In groups of four issue students' answers to a crossword puzzle. The group then breaks into pairs with one pair taking the down answers and the other taking the across answers. In their pairs the students have a predetermined period of time to write and organise the clues that are needed to arrive at the answers they have been given. The group then reforms and each pair take turns to give and guess the clues. More and more clues can be given if a pair has difficulty.

Stand and Share: *this is a suitable activity for sharing information with others so students can learn from each other.* Students work in groups to complete an activity. Each member of the group needs to be able to explain the work done. Ask all groups to stand. Call on one student randomly to state something they have learnt from the work. Others in the class who had the same idea sit down, while those in the class who have a different idea remain standing. Continue until all students are seated.

Two Stay Two Stray: *here students work in groups of four to complete a project.* Once finished groups nominate two members who will stay with the work and answer questions about it and two members who will stray to other groups and investigate their work to see if they can gain ideas which will improve their own group's work. The groups then reunite and consider any suggestions the two who stayed have to improve or add to the group's work.

Roam the Room: similar to the previous activity but all members in the group roam the room collecting ideas.

Check and Coach: *this is useful as an end of topic activity to review or reteach new concepts.* Students work alone to revise or master new material then continue this process in groups of four. The group decides on a new way to present the material, e.g. an article of text may be transformed into a bullet point summary, concept map, pictorial representations, etc. Once the students have transformed the material into the new format, they check that all group members understand it and can answer questions about it. The group then divides into two pairs and joins up with a pair from another group. One member of each pair then explains the work to the other pair without the aid of notes. The other member of that pair holds the notes to check that their partner is accurate in their explanation.

Role Cards

Project Manager :

You are responsible for completing the final written report of the project, making sure everyone has contributed and coordinating everyone's ideas.

Coordination Manager :

You are responsible for collecting and returning materials, keeping in touch with the teacher, making sure the group meets deadlines, ensuring the group is on-task, assisting the project manager.

Cooperation Manager :

You are responsible for evaluating the group's success with social skills, encouraging a good team spirit, monitoring noise levels, ensuring all group members fulfil their role, assisting the artistic manager.

Artistic Manager :

You are responsible for organising the layout of the project, drawing headings, borders and pictures, coordinating everyone's artistic ideas.

Director :

You help the group make fair decisions and act as the group's spokesperson. You edit and proof read the group's work, read out any necessary instructions, take notes for the group.

46

Peer-and Cross-age Tutoring Ideas

Key Steps

1. Assess the need for a peer-tutor programme in a particular curriculum area.
2. Communicate the rationale for the programme to other staff.
3. Prepare the learning activity and accompanying resources.
4. Decide on a suitable teaching approach that has simple specific steps for tutors to follow.
5. Select and train appropriate students to act as tutors. Explain the idea of the programme, teach session routines, explain the learning task, teach tutoring skills such as those in the **Study Buddy Job Description**, and explain record keeping that needs to be completed.
6. Assign tutors to students.
7. Timetable the teaching sessions and implement the programme.
8. Monitor the process and student progress throughout the programme.
9. Evaluate the effectiveness in terms of student progress.
10. Reward tutor participation.

Key Elements

- Teaching needs to occur in a collaborative atmosphere in which value is placed on the tutor's ability to develop the students' skills.
- Active listening is used by the tutor to confirm student's understanding.
- The tutor extends the student's ability by attempting tasks which are beyond the range of their independent ability, but are achievable with support.
- As the student develops competency and skills they are encouraged to take more responsibility for completing the learning task independently.

Possible Applications in Core Curriculum Areas

- **Reading**: the tutor can listen to the student read a book, assist with word recognition and question for comprehension. Alternatively use a system for non-fiction which requires the students to read a passage aloud, summarise the passage in ten words then predict what the next passage is about.
- **Story writing**: tutors can assist with developing story ideas, edit the student's writing for spelling, punctuation, and grammar, and extend their vocabulary by suggesting synonyms.
- **Handwriting**: the tutor can model the formation of letters and guide the student in practising these.
- **Spelling**: tutors can serve to pre- and post-test list words and aid the student to memorise words.
- **Maths**: the tutor can model maths problems and guide the student as they practice or help the learner memorise times tables etc by using flash cards.
- **Science / History / Geography / PSHE**: the tutor and student complete a worksheet together and then the student completes a similar sheet independently.

④ Teacher-directed Teaching and Instructions

 KEY IDEA: to motivate the student to sustain attention during teacher-directed teaching times and to accurately follow teacher instructions.

Points to consider

- Interact with the student and use the student's name frequently.

- Actively involve the student in the lesson, e.g. ask them to write the classes' ideas on the board or help set up the audio visual equipment.

- Consider allowing the student to play with something in their hands while listening, e.g. modelling clay.

- When giving instructions stand close, face the student, and make frequent eye contact. Try to be at the same level physically as the student while using relevant gestures as you deliver the instructions.

- Instructions should be short, specific and direct, and given only one step at a time and never issued in multi-steps. If necessary, tape record instructions for the student to replay.

- Illustrate and write instructions in addition to giving them in spoken form.

- Write commonly repeated instructions on flash cards: stop work / pack up.

- Ask the student to paraphrase the instructions into their own words and check their understanding frequently.

Implementation Steps

1. Complete the **Instruction Comic Strip** when issuing unfamiliar instructions to the student. This entails writing in the instruction, graphically depicting it using a simple drawing, and then having the student briefly record their understanding of it. The student then ticks off each instruction as they complete it.

2. Use the **Flash Cards** provided for commonly used instructions or prepare your own. Either Velcro these to a piece of card or place them on the student's desk in the order they are required to follow them. Laminate these so they last longer.

Instruction Comic Strip

✓

Written Instruction	Picture of Instruction	Your Version	Tick when Completed

Instruction Flash Cards

Line up outside

Get ready for the next subject

Put on your PE gear

Sit on the mat

Write the work in your book

Read quietly

Get out your books

Find a partner

Put the equipment away

Pack up

Hand in your work

Tidy your area

Work with your Study Buddy

Glue this in your book

Put up your chair

Complete the work sheet

Colour this in

Work with your teacher aid

Get the equipment ready

Turn to page___

Go to Room___

Put this in your bag

Choose a library book

Get into groups

5 Organisation

 KEY IDEA: to help the student develop strategies that will help them be better organised.

Points to consider

- Model good organisation yourself. Make the strategies you use visible to the students.

- Before implementing any intervention for organisation make sure that students with ADHD can tell the time and read calendars and timetables.

- Demonstrate the value of organisational skills by giving the student (indeed the whole class) five minutes at the end of each day to prepare for the following day. They can organise their desks and books, review their timetable, etc. Alternatively give the student five minutes at the beginning of each day to get out everything they need for the day ahead.

- Give students a visual representation of the class timetable and a list of supplies needed each day. This can be kept on an open shelf which will prevent them from wasting time by "desk digging". By using clockfaces on the timetable to indicate the time subjects start you can also assist them to learn the skill of telling time.

- To alleviate difficulty with transitions provide a five minute warning like, "Five minutes until your project must be handed in," or use a visual cue such as a red card or holding up your hand.

- For each learning area have a different book with a different coloured cover. Keep them all in a zippered pocket/s that can also take loose paper too. This way everything is kept together. Colour coding is a very useful strategy to use when teaching students with ADHD.

- Encourage the student to use a calendar to indicate due dates of classroom assignments and record upcoming school events.

- Monitor the student's system of organisation daily for at least six weeks to establish good routines.

- Students with ADHD need structured lists, reminders, and rituals wherever possible. If a student has difficulty following an established routine in any particular area provide them with a written list of what is expected.

- Provide a diary to write down items of importance.

- Students with ADHD often complete their homework but forget to hand it in or lose it. Encourage the student to place homework in their book bag and actively remind them to hand it in at the beginning of each day.

- Where possible don't allow things to go home. Instead provide duplicate copies for home use.
- Conduct regular desk checks and issue incentives for students who have a tidy desk.
- To ease classroom clean ups and help the student efficiently access classroom supplies use pictures to label commonly used things e.g. scissors, crayons etc.

Implementation Steps

1. Create a **Visual Timetable** by using the **Pictures** and template provided to reflect your class schedule. Draw in the hands on the clock faces to indicate the starting times of each subject.

2. Write in any necessary additions and attach the **List of Daily Supplies** and visual timetable to the student's desk.

3. Ask the student's parents to cover each of their books in a different colour and buy zippered pockets and a book bag so all books can be kept in it. Provide the students with the **Book Labels** and have them illustrate and colour the labels before attaching them to each book. Place two writing instruments in each pocket.

4. Complete the necessary sections so the **Perpetual Calendar** is accurate for the current month. Glue this into the front cover of each book. Photocopy the **Due Date Pictures** onto red card and each time you indicate an assignment date have the student glue the card on the appropriate date. Allow the student to personalise these with stickers and artwork and record upcoming school events.

5. Assign a competent student to monitor the student's system of organisation. Place a list of all the student's necessary school supplies in their book bag and ask the peer to check daily for six weeks to make sure that everything is present. Each time the student achieves good daily organisation issue them with an **Outstanding Organisation** or **Trophy of Tidiness** award which they can redeem for an incentive once a predetermined number have been collected.

6. Complete the **Routine Chart**, if necessary, for all learning areas. This lists expected steps and can be attached to the inside cover of the relevant book. Alert them to prepare students for the next piece of work when they have five minutes remaining by showing them a **Transition Red Card**.

7. Use the **Diary** for recording homework, reminders, writing upcoming events, etc. Work collaboratively with the student and parents by asking them to read and sign it each evening. Make sure it is returned to the book bag along with any homework that is completed. Also provide duplicate copies of resources to send home remembering to complete a list as a record of what you have sent home.

8. Conduct random desk checks weekly and leave students a **Trophy of Tidiness** voucher each time they meet the required standard of tidiness. Have students place these into a box and draw out one each week to receive a small prize.

9. Photocopy the applicable **Picture Labels** onto different coloured cards and attach to items through the room.

Visual Timetable

Time	MONDAY	TUESDAY	WEDNESDAY	THURSDAY	FRIDAY

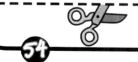

Visual Timetable Pictures – Examples

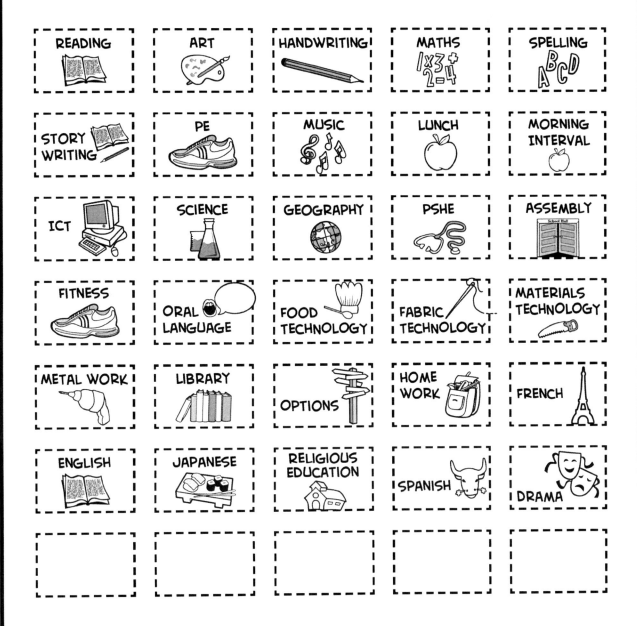

List of Daily Supplies for: _____

Day : _____

Stationery items

- ☐ Ruler
- ☐ Glue stick
- ☐ Refill paper
- ☐ Red pen
- ☐ Black pen
- ☐ Scissors
- ☐ Pencil
- ☐ Rubber
- ☐ Compass
- ☐ Protractor

Textbooks

- ☐ Dictionary

Subject work books

- ☐ Design and Technology
- ☐ English
- ☐ Maths
- ☐ Art and Design
- ☐ Citizenship
- ☐ Science
- ☐ Geography
- ☐ PSHE

Other items

- ☐ PE gear
- ☐ Swimming trunks
- ☐ _____
- ☐ _____
- ☐ _____
- ☐ _____
- ☐ _____
- ☐ _____

Book Labels

Name _____

Address _____

Phone number _____

Teacher's name _____

Class room _____

Name _____

Address _____

Phone number _____

Teacher's name _____

Class room _____

Name _____

Address _____

Phone number _____

Teacher's name _____

Class room _____

Name _____

Address _____

Phone number _____

Teacher's name _____

Class room _____

Name _____

Address _____

Phone number _____

Teacher's name _____

Class room _____

Name _____

Address _____

Phone number _____

Teacher's name _____

Class room _____

Name _____

Address _____

Phone number _____

Teacher's name _____

Class room _____

Name _____

Address _____

Phone number _____

Teacher's name _____

Class room _____

Perpetual Calendar

Calendar for: _____

Month : _____

Week : _____

MONDAY	TUESDAY	WEDNESDAY	THURSDAY	FRIDAY

Due Date Pictures

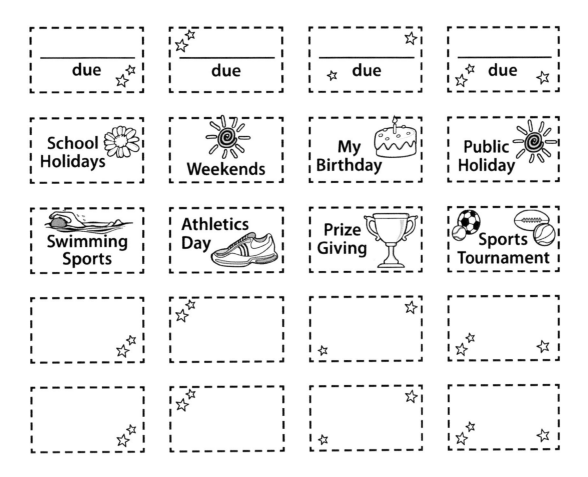

_____ due ✩	✩ _____ due	✩ _____ due ✩	✩ _____ due ✩
School Holidays	Weekends	My Birthday	Public Holiday
Swimming Sports	Athletics Day	Prize Giving	Sports Tournament
✩	✩	✩ ✩	✩ ✩
✩ ✩	✩	✩ ✩	✩ ✩

Routine Chart

Routine for :

1	
2	
3	
4	
5	
6	
7	
8	
9	

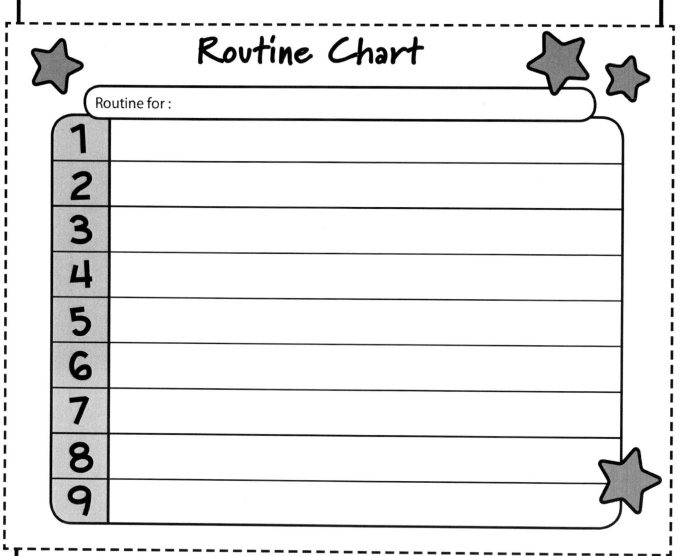

Transition Red Card

In **five minutes** we will be starting a new subject. Finish what you are doing, pack up and get ready for the next subject on your timetable.

5 Minutes

Diary

1. List all the things you need to remember each day.
2. Rank them in order of importance.
3. Tick the box to show they have been completed.

Reminder	Rank 1 - 5	Tick when completed	Notes and Parent Signature
MONDAY			Signed : _____
TUESDAY			Signed : _____
WEDNESDAY			Signed : _____
THURSDAY			Signed : _____
FRIDAY			Signed : _____

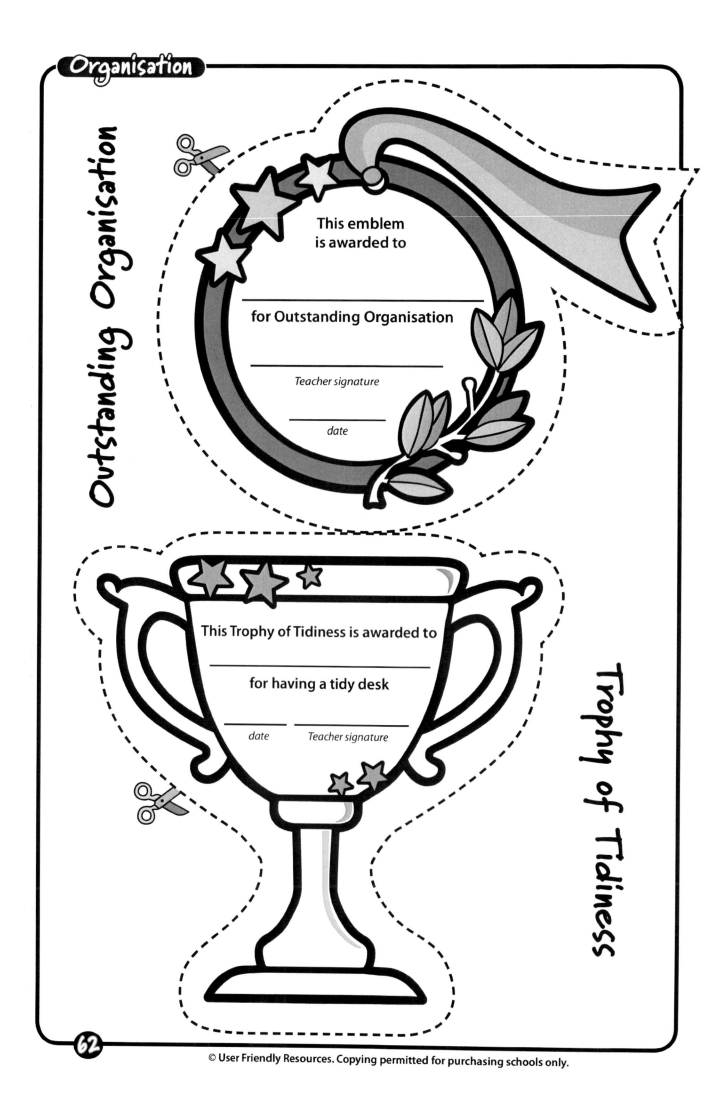

Outstanding Organisation

This emblem
is awarded to

_____

for Outstanding Organisation

_____

Teacher signature

_____

date

This Trophy of Tidiness is awarded to

_____

for having a tidy desk

_____   _____
date   *Teacher signature*

Trophy of Tidiness

Picture Labels

SCISSORS 	CRAYONS 	GLUE
MARKED BOOKS 	BOOKS FOR MARKING 	ART PAPER 
SCRAP PAPER 	LIBRARY BOOK RETURNS 	MATHS EQUIPMENT 
ART EQUIPMENT 	SCIENCE EQUIPMENT 	LUNCH ORDERS

6 Teacher Relationship

 KEY IDEA: to establish a rapport with the student that helps to foster a positive relationship and leads to an effective learning climate.

Points to consider

- The nature of ADHD means performance is variable. On low performance days the student is not just "not trying"; it is part of the disorder.

- Use parents and teacher aides in the classroom whenever possible. This will help to achieve a lower student to adult ratio.

- Develop a rapport with the student and treat them with respect. This is fundamental to working effectively with students who have ADHD. Often they will work to please others that they respect.

- Ask yourself if your actions will bring you closer to the student or push you further apart. Avoid criticising, blaming, complaining, nagging, threatening, punishing and bribing. Endeavour to listen, support, encourage, respect, trust, accept and negotiate.

- Reassure, encourage and compliment the student frequently and speak softly in a non-threatening manner during all interactions. Students with ADHD need lots of encouragement as they have accumulated many self-doubts. However try to be discreet when praising the student by using verbal, visual, or gestural acknowledgements.

- Correspondingly instigate and implement private cues and visual signals to moderate behaviour. This helps to avoid direct confrontation and public humiliation.

- Notice the student's moods. Alleviate pressure by making time to talk to them.

- Listen to the student's point of view when they encounter difficulties and ensure they understand that you are there to help them.

- Actively implement practices in the classroom which will help build the student's self-esteem.

Implementation Steps

1. Educate yourself about the ADHD condition by attending courses and reading the wealth of literature that is available. In so doing you will be better able to keep a positive perspective on days when the student is particularly challenging.

2. Enlist the support of your colleagues both formally and informally. Discuss difficulties you are having with the student and successes you have had. Request assistance when needed from the school leadership team either in the form of extra help in the classroom from a teacher aide or by having an ADHD-free day. The student could be assigned to do other things such as help in the office once every so often.

3. Develop a relationship with the student by getting to know them as an individual. Allocate five minutes each day to discuss their interests outside of school and try to greet the student on arrival and after breaks. Make an effort to wink, smile or touch the student's shoulders as frequently as possible.

4. Photocopy the **Teacher Interaction Tokens** onto two different coloured cards. Use these to monitor the type of interactions you have with the student. Each time you speak to the student put the relevant card into a jar. At the end of the day you will have a very clear idea of the predominant type of interactions you have.

5. Acknowledge positive behaviour as early in the day as possible and make encouragement specific, say, " I like the way you …" Catch the student being 'good' in their achievements, applying effort, positive interactions, or sustaining attention. Aim to acknowledge positive behaviour more regularly than inappropriate behaviour, ideally on a 3: 1 ratio. Develop private gestures, for example thumbs up to indicate well done, or touch an ear to direct the student to listen.

6. Allow a 15-minute stress break during the day to do a quiet activity during times of high stress or if you notice the student's mood has deteriorated. Following this break take time to speak privately with the student. It may be helpful to initiate the conversation by saying, "I noticed you did not look very happy before, would you care to talk about it?"

7. Following an incident of difficulty in which the student has responded negatively have them fill in the **Hassle Log** as a means of getting their point of view. Once this is completed discuss the incident in a non-judgmental manner. If a consequence must be applied phrase this by saying, "I understand how you felt. Unfortunately, because you handled the situation in that way the consequence is …"

8. Implement ideas that appeal to you from the **Self-esteem Ideas** provided. Always try to engage in some strategy that is designed to build a positive self-concept in your students.

Teacher Interaction Tokens

POSITIVE
INTERACTION

NEGATIVE
INTERACTION

POSITIVE
INTERACTION

NEGATIVE
INTERACTION

POSITIVE
INTERACTION

NEGATIVE
INTERACTION

POSITIVE
INTERACTION

NEGATIVE
INTERACTION

Hassle Log

Name _____ **Date** _____

This is what happened

- ☐ Someone ordered me about
- ☐ Someone did something I didn't like
- ☐ My work was too hard
- ☐ Other _____
- ☐ Someone started an argument with me
- ☐ I did something wrong
- ☐ Someone didn't listen to me

This is when it happened

- ☐ Class time
- ☐ Playtime
- ☐ After school
- ☐ Lunch time
- ☐ Before school
- ☐ Other _____

This is how I felt

☐ Burning angry   ☐ Really angry   ☐ Angry   ☐ Quite angry   ☐ Other _____

This is who made me feel this way

☐ Student   ☐ Teacher   ☐ Staff member   ☐ My friend   ☐ Other _____

This is what I did

- ☐ Hit back
- ☐ Kicked
- ☐ Yelled
- ☐ Swore
- ☐ Argued
- ☐ Cried
- ☐ Ran away
- ☐ Went silent
- ☐ Hurt myself
- ☐ Hid somewhere
- ☐ Got revenge
- ☐ Broke something
- ☐ Other _____

This is how I think I handled the situation

☐ Very well   ☐ OK   ☐ Very badly

The outcome of the situation was _____

_____

_____

This is what I would do differently next time _____

_____

_____

Self-esteem Ideas

- **Happy note box:** put a shoebox and pencil in a prominent area of the room. Encourage students to notice each other doing good deeds then record it and post it in the box. On a Friday read aloud all the names posted and their deeds and draw out one name for a prize.

- **Compliment chart:** create a chart with students' names down one side and room to place compliments cards on the other. Create cards with compliments on them, e.g. friendly, kind, considerate, thoughtful, good sense of humour, good friend, fun to be with, generous, gentle, brave, caring, etc. Randomly assign each student the name of a classmate and ask them to stick a relevant compliment card beside the name. Display in a prominent place.

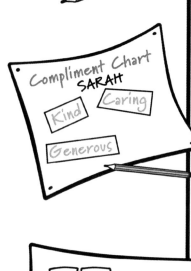

- **Achievement certificates:** cut up a certificate into several bits for each student. Have a piece of cardboard which matches the certificate size displayed with each students' name on it. Each time they achieve something or make an improvement they glue a piece of the certificate onto their card.

- **The virtue vine:** devote a wall in the classroom and place a vine stem on it for each student. Each time you notice the student display a positive quality, write it on a leaf and attach it to their vine.

- **Baby face:** ask students to bring a baby photo to school. Display two at a time each with strips of paper around them outlining things about the student in the present, e.g. is good at maths, fun to play with. Let the class try and guess who the photo shows.

⑦ Parent Relationship

KEY IDEA: to establish and maintain an effective working relationship with the student's parents.

Points to consider

- Hold regular parent conferences to complete learning and behaviour programme goals. Enlisting parent support is essential for the success of any intervention, as there needs to be an effective partnership between families, schools and other specialists. Planning interventions for the student should be a team activity founded on respect for the options and choices of all involved.

- Set up home/ school notebooks. This shows the student that both parties are working together to help them. It also provides a record of daily behaviour that highlights any changes in behaviour which parents need to be aware of that may be linked to medication issues.

- Send positive notes and progress reports home frequently.

- Help parents to establish a friendship plan to encourage out-of-school friendships. For friendships to develop the student needs to have a physical proximity to peers and opportunities for interaction. They need to be aware of the principles of friendship and have a respect for diversity. They also need to be competent in the skills that support friendship such as a positive interaction style, areas of compatibility, taking the perspective of others, sharing and providing support, trustworthiness and loyalty, and conflict resolution. Friendships need to be given time to evolve and students need opportunities where adults are not involved for genuine reciprocal friendships to eventuate.

Implementation Steps

1. Schedule a parent conference as early in the year as possible and invite any other relevant specialists. At this meeting you should aim to complete the **Individual Behaviour Plan** and **Individual Education Plan**. Set a date at the meeting to evaluate the behaviour plan and write the next one. This should ideally be done each term.

2. Glue the **Home/ School Comments** page into each alternate page of the diary issued to the student (see the *Organisation* section) and complete this daily.

3. Keep a pile of the **Positive Progress Reports** and **Positive Notes** on your desk and send these home as regularly as possible.

4. If parents are implementing a friendship plan, talk to them about the need for their student to practise making arrangements and offering invitations. They should plan a structured recreational activity, and teach friendship skills in which the student needs guidance.

69

Individual Behaviour Plan

Name

Date

Review date

Strengths/ skills/ positive behaviours

Challenging behaviours to be managed

What is the function of this behaviour or what is the student trying to communicate?

Learning objective

Prevention strategies

Teaching strategies for replacement behaviour

Incentives

Consequences

Resources needed

Responsibilities

Individual Education Plan

Name _____

School _____

Date of meeting _____

People present _____

Date of birth _____

Class _____

Review date _____

Curriculum area	Current skill level	Specific learning outcome / goal	Strategies and resources to achieve this	Person responsible for implementation	Evaluation

Evaluation of Individual Behaviour Plan

Evaluation of Individual Behaviour Plan

Goals set

Strategies implemented to achieve goals

Goals achieved and progress made

Reasons for progress

Goals not achieved

Possible reasons for non-achievement

What those involved found successful

What those involved think could be done differently

Strategies to continue to maintain progress

Other issues discussed

Support agencies available

 Parent Relationship

Home/School Comments

Home School Notebook

Day _____ Date _____

Target behaviours

1 _____

2 _____

3 _____

	General behaviour at school			Target behaviours		
8:30 – 10:30	☺	😐	☹	☺	😐	☹
INTERVAL	☺	😐	☹	☺	😐	☹
11:00 – 12:30	☺	😐	☹	☺	😐	☹
LUNCHTIME	☺	😐	☹	☺	😐	☹
1:30 – 3:00	☺	😐	☹	☺	😐	☹

" Did I make good choices in the classroom, in the playground, relating to other people?"

Student comment _____

_____

Student signature _____

Teacher comment _____

_____

Teacher signature _____

Parent comment _____

_____

Parent signature _____

Progress Reports and Positive Notes

Progress Report

A message from the teacher.

Dear : _____

Just a brief note to let you know that

_____

Has made progress with _____

_____

_____

Signed   *date*

Positive Note

A message from the teacher.

Dear : _____

Just a brief note to let you know that you can be

proud of _____

for _____

_____

Signed   *date*

⑧ Managing Behaviour

 KEY IDEA: to implement strategies that will help minimise impulsive behaviour and foster positive behaviour.

Points to consider

- Model the expected behaviour, establish and maintain routines, and ensure the student has easy access to resources that they frequently use.

- Use well-defined, specific rules, which are frequently reinforced and followed up. These should set firm limits and make clear your expectations. Your behaviour standards must be realistic and you need to ensure any negative consequences are not excessive. Present the rules in visual form, along with the consequences of non-adherence and incentives for adhering to the rules. When applying consequences for both positive and negative behaviours you must do it immediately.

- Review the rules daily and before beginning every activity. Instead of phrasing them as rules add a positive focus by calling them R U's: Are you … in your seat?

- Ignore minor misdemeanours and focus on the positives.

- Students with ADHD are drawn to high stimuli and need to be taught to choose them wisely. Rather than reprimand, point out the alternative choices the student could have made, as this helps to clarify your expectations. In addition, aside from indicating to the student what behaviours are unacceptable, teach the expected acceptable behaviours. Acceptable behaviours need to be clearly defined and monitored. Feedback should be immediate and regular.

- Use teacher-proximity to moderate behaviour and roam the room frequently.

- Introduce a delay time before students answer a question to encourage reasoning and deter impulsive answering.

- Conduct an analysis of the antecedents and consequences of inappropriate behaviour. This allows you to determine what classroom aspects precipitate the behaviour and what consequences reinforce it. Consider the behaviour's duration, intensity, range, and whether it is situationally diverse.

- Implement short-term behaviour contracts that focus on only two to three goals at a time. Include the student in formulating them by using a teacher-created menu from which students can select goals. The criteria for success must be clearly defined, e.g. *Work silently for 15 minutes.* Remember that any intervention must allow for early success or the student won't buy into it, so choose achievable goals.

- Variety is essential in maintaining the effectiveness of behaviour systems. At least once a term modify your established systems to promote positive behaviour.

75

- Incentives are a powerful motivator for students with ADHD, as these students tend not to be responsive to intangible reinforcement. However, any incentive systems used need to be changed frequently, as they lose their power once the novelty value diminishes. Always ensure incentives are immediate, accessible and highly stimulating. Negotiate with the student to identify the incentives they want and record them on an incentive menu. Always pair verbal praise with all concrete incentives, as eventually this will allow you to wean the student onto an internalised reward system.

- Teach self-monitoring by using a rating scale which prompts a move to internal evaluation of behaviour.

- If you would prefer to introduce less formal behaviour systems, you might consider trying one of these ideas:

    - On Monday write the word SURPRISE on the board. Erase a letter for any misbehaviour. If any letters remain on Friday the student earns a surprise.

    - Make a hangman out of cardboard and paperclips. Construct it piece by piece for any misbehaviour. If it is fully constructed implement the agreed upon consequence.

    - Issue Get Out of Trouble Free coupons as incentives and allow student to redeem them if they forget homework or indulge in any minor misbehaviours.

- Establish a Time Out system. This is beneficial for reducing major disruption in class. However you need to ensure that the student does not use it as a strategy for avoiding schoolwork by asking them to complete any work missed while in Time Out. If the student is more prone to minor misbehaviour such as being noisy, use a noise meter system with red, orange and green indicators. If it hits red the student is to be silent for one minute for each year of age e.g. ten years old = ten minutes.

- On field trips ensure the student has a name badge with their home and school phone number on it. Use a buddy system and never let the student be at the back of the line as they are prone to wandering off.

Implementation Steps

1. Review your class schedule to see whether you have implemented and maintained routines in as many day-to-day areas as possible. Reflect on the classroom layout map to determine that the student's access to resources is not hindered by obstacles which could precipitate negative behaviour.

2. Enlarge the **Behaviour Chart** to A3 size and complete each section in collaboration with the class before displaying it in a prominent place on the classroom wall. Review the chart before every lesson initially to prompt students about what is expected. Try to include this review in the beginning of day routine.

3. Ensure your interactions with the student are mainly positive by using the strategy mentioned in the **Teacher Relationship** section of this resource. Choose your battles by ignoring minor transgressions. Acknowledge the positive behaviour of nearby students instead.

4. If you need to reprimand the student, ask them "What could you choose to do next time instead of…." This helps clarify your expectations and teaches the student to consider an alternative behaviour. Try to give regular, immediate feedback to the student on their efforts with new behaviours.

5. Ensure the student is always in close physical proximity to you to deter inappropriate behaviour.

6. Complete the **ABC** sheet and **Event Record** for two weeks before implementing any behaviour system. This will provide you with a record of behaviours that are of concern and allow you to see any patterns that may exist. Where possible alleviate any of these behaviours by making environmental changes.

7. Complete the **Goal Menu** by recording the behaviours that you would like the student to work on. Ensure you phrase these in a positive way. Suggest the alternative behaviour you would like the student to show. You might consider including: Be on time to class; Have all my equipment organised; Pay attention in class; Follow instructions given by the teacher; Do tasks when asked in the way asked; Don't talk in class when the teacher requires silence; Don't call out, make noise or argue; Don't misuse equipment; Don't waste time or get behind in my work; Stay in my seat. Enlarge to A3.

8. Complete the **Short-term Token Economy Contract** with two to three behaviour goals and collaborate with the student to complete the **Incentive Menu** from which they will choose. Plot the student's points daily on the contracts graph so they have a visual record of their behaviour. Allow them to choose a low-level incentive on days they have had success and a higher level incentive once they have altered the behaviour for five consecutive days. Remember to use verbal praise each time an incentive is earned. This contract employs a token economy approach in which you give tokens for appropriate behaviour. These can then be exchanged for incentives and privileges. Enlarge to A3. Attach a points value to goals before starting the contract.

9. Once the novelty of this dissipates, implement the **Response Cost Contract** in which you allocate points at beginning of the day and the student loses points for not meeting expectations. At the end of the day they continue to exchange their points for an incentive, or bank them towards a higher level incentive.

10. At the end of each day also ask the student to evaluate their success towards achieving each goal by completing the **Self-monitoring Rating Scale** and then plot their results on the graph.

11. Continue to use the voucher system provided throughout this resource for behaviours you are trying to encourage that have not been specified on the contracts. Implement any other informal behaviour system you feel will be advantageous.

12. If a student is being highly disruptive *ask* him or her to rectify their behaviour, and if they do not, *tell* the student to rectify their behaviour. If the student is still being unduly disruptive, place the relevant **Time Out** card on their desk as a cue for them to leave the room and report to the designated area. Have the student stay there for one minute per year of age. When they return It is essential to discuss with the student what went wrong and how they can prevent a future reoccurrence... you might discuss the problem with the student by saying, "This is what I needed from you, this is what I saw you doing, this is what I want you to do now – can you do it?" If a student refuses to go to Time Out say, "I'll give you two minutes to think about going or there will be more serious consequences."

13. Complete the **Name Badge** and place inside a name badge clip or laminate and safety pin in preparation for any field trips.

Behaviour Chart

These rules help you to choose to behave in a positive way by knowing what is expected.	These incentives help you to develop positive behaviours by encouraging you to follow the rules.	These consequences are stated so you know what will happen if you choose to break the rules.
Rules	**Incentives**	**Consequences**
1	1	1
2	2	2
3	3	3
4	4	4
5	5	5

Analysis of Antecedents and Consequences (ABC Sheet)

Student name _____

Teacher _____

Behaviours of concern

1 _____

2 _____

3 _____

Date and Day	Time, Subject and Setting	Who it involved	What led up to or contributed to the behaviour?	Describe the behaviour of concern specifically	What occurred immediately following the behaviour	What consequences were implemented?

Factors for consideration

Student's characteristics	Parenting practices	Family issues	Critical events/traumas	Other	Teachers' opinion on why the student behaves this way

Event Record

Name _____ Teacher _____ Date _____

Tick boxes to gather data regarding the frequency of the behaviour.

Give a 1-5 rating to indicate the intensity of the behaviour in relation to how it effects the student's teacher or peers.

		Out of seat or wandering	Talking to others	Not listening to instructions	Not paying attention	Disorganised	Non compliance	Annoying others	Inappropriately loud	Calling out	Off task	Other	Intensity
Morning	Teacher directed work												
	Group work												
	Independent work												
	Other												
Afternoon	Teacher directed work												
	Group work												
	Independent work												
	Other												
	Totals												

Goal Menu and Incentive Menu

Goal Menu

Value

Incentive Menu

Short-term Token Economy Contract

Name _____

Date _____ Room _____

Goal behaviours	Monday			Tuesday			Wednesday			Thursday			Friday		
	AM	Lunch	PM	AM	Lunch	PM	AM	Lunch	PM	AM	Lunch	PM	AM	Lunch	PM
Total for day (graph)															
Total for week															

We agree to the terms stated in this contract and will each be responsible for completing our part.

Home incentive _____ Parent signature _____

School incentive _____ Teacher signature _____

Each day I will choose to try and meet these goal behaviours. If I succeed I will get the agreed points awarded. My teacher will bank these points each day. At the end of each day I will get the choice of selecting something from the incentive menu or saving up my points to choose bigger items.

Student signature _____

Results Graph for Week Ending _____

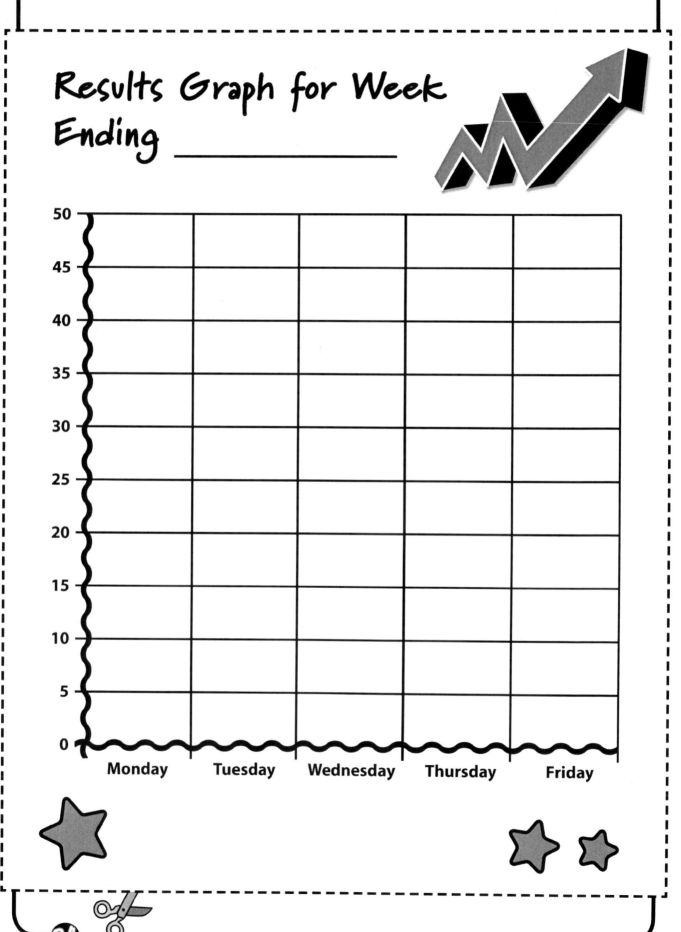

	Monday	Tuesday	Wednesday	Thursday	Friday

(y-axis: 0, 5, 10, 15, 20, 25, 30, 35, 40, 45, 50)

Response Cost Contract

To get the most out of school I agree to:

1 _____

2 _____

3 _____

For each behaviour I do not meet I will lose 10 points.

Signature _____

		Monday	Tuesday	Wednesday	Thursday	Friday
Date __/__/__	Points I begin with					
	Points deducted					
Date __/__/__	Points I begin with					
	Points deducted					
Date __/__/__	Points I begin with					
	Points deducted					
Date __/__/__	Points I begin with					
	Points deducted					
Date __/__/__	Points I begin with					
	Points deducted					
	Total for day					

Self-monitoring Rating Scale

Student _____ Day _____

Behaviour goals : 1 _____

2 _____

3 _____

Time of day	Comment	Self behaviour rating 1 - poor 5 - great	Consequence or incentive
Morning			
Middle			
Afternoon			

Total _____

Today I felt 😊 😐 ☹ about my learning	I felt my attitude today was 😊 😐 ☹
I felt 😊 😐 ☹ about the work I completed today	My behaviour today was 😊 😐 ☹
Tomorrow I want to try harder at:	Today my teacher thinks:

Time Out System

COURTEOUS	COOPERATIVE	CAREFUL
COMMITTED	CONSIDERATE	IN CONTROL

 You were choosing not to be...

Please go to _____ **for**
___ minutes and _____ **.**

Name Badge

HI MY NAME IS ...

Name : _____

Home phone number : _____

School phone number : _____

⑨ Peer Relationships

KEY IDEA: to implement strategies that will assist the student to establish and maintain positive peer relationships.

Points to consider

- Establish a "Students with ADHD" support group on a school-wide basis to give students with ADHD an arena in which to discuss their experiences within an accepting environment.

- Explain the ADHD condition and the student's needs to classroom peers to help understanding. Discuss this with parents first to gain their consent.

- Establish a safe environment and never allow name-calling or teasing. This is particularly important, as students with ADHD are hypersensitive to rejection. Strive to recognise the talents as well as the weaknesses of the student and develop strong positive expectations for the student's success while leading the class to do the same.

- Never punish the whole class for the student with ADHD's behaviour.

- Provide leadership and social interaction opportunities.

- Target and practise social skills before upcoming events and take time to reflect on these afterwards. Establish social behaviour goals in conjunction with academic goals.

- Teach necessary interaction skills by providing opportunities for guided observation in the playground to focus on the social skills of the student's peers. Accompany the student in the playground and observe and discuss how others initiate games, cooperate in games, respond to rejection, deal with being alone etc.

- If the student tends to encounter difficulties in the playground, plan what they will do during breaks like who they will play with before they go out. Depending on age, it may be helpful to establish play groups with socially competent peers and activities that stress cooperation and interaction. Often ADHD students play better with students older than themselves, as the roles are more clearly defined. Have a buddy system in the playground and structure playground activities.

- At lunchtime have the student check in with the duty member every 10 minutes and simplify playground interactions by restricting playground areas to those near supervision.

Implementation Steps

1. Assign a suitable member of staff to establish the ADHD support group and hold meetings twice a term. The purpose of forming an ADHD support group is to provide students with an opportunity to meet others in the school community who have ADHD, and to gain from this a sense of mutual support. It is important that membership and participation in the group is voluntary and flexible in that it does not require a fixed duration of membership. While the members of the group should have the power to define the focus and purpose, an agenda might entail sharing the experience of having ADHD, sharing any issues and concerns about ADHD, sharing strategies to overcome problems related to ADHD, and perhaps the opportunity to learn relevant skills.

2. Conduct the **Respecting Individual Difference Lessons** with the whole class to help peers gain an understanding of ADHD with the whole class as early in the first term. These two books also provide an excellent platform for discussion. *Jumping Johnny Get Back to Work: A Child's Guide to ADHD,* by Gordon, M. (1991) GSI Publications; and *Eukee the Jumpy Jumpy Elephant, by Corman, C., Trevino, E., (1995), Specialty Press.*

3. Ensure your interactions with the student foster a positive relationship so that you are modelling the value of respect to the student's peers. Remember that the students will follow your example.

4. Assess the social climate of your classroom regularly, and if necessary implement cooperative learning or team building activities. Assign special responsibilities to the student and ensure the peer group can generally see the student being reflected in a positive light.

5. Role play the etiquette of any school events that the student could benefit from learning.

6. Ensure you have included social behaviour goals in IEPs and on the previously mentioned goal menu, and where relevant complete the **Social Behaviour Goals** sheet with the student.

7. Conduct some **Guided Playground Observation** sessions with the student using the guide sheet as a focus.

8. Use the **Playground Plan** sheet to help plan what the student will do on breaks and clarify the behavioural expectations.

Lessons to Support Respecting Individual Differences

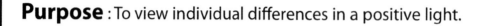

Purpose : To view individual differences in a positive light.

Format

- Establish ground rules such as noise levels, strategies for calling class back, social and behavioural expectations.

- **The human domino game:** This game is designed for students to find out what they have in common. Students have to form a chain by talking to one another and in some way finding a match. For example, George starts the chain and then Frank stands beside him because they both support the same football team. Michael stands beside Frank because they have the same middle name, etc. Play the game in groups of eight to begin with, then attempt it with the whole class.

- **Class discussion:** define what it means to be the same as others.

- **Game of uses:** students are given an object and must try to come up with different uses for that object.

- **Machine team game:** in groups of four students are given a machine to form each person in the team must be a different part of the machine.

- **Class discussion:** discuss and define what it means to be different from others.

- **Hot seat:** the teacher takes the role of a character from "same world" where everyone is the same, and then a character from "different world". Students ask the teacher questions in character to discover the advantages and disadvantages of living in each world.

- **Class poster:** each student is issued two cards, one with the title *It's great to be the same because …* and the other *It's great to be different because…* they complete the sentence with one idea then attach them to a class poster to demonstrate what they have learnt.

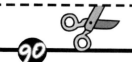

LESSON 2

Purpose : To develop an understanding of individual difference and an acknowledgement that people have skills in some areas and needs in others.

Format

- **Employ an expert:** this is a game designed for students to find out from each other what unique things they can do. Ask students to list three areas that they have a lot of knowledge in e.g. dinosaurs, rugby, etc, and three areas they have skills in, e.g. drawing horses, scoring goals. Once completed, issue students with paper and ask them to design a poster advertising their skills. Display these around the room. Next have students list one thing they would like to learn more about and one skill they would like to learn. Have the students roam the room and look at the posters to find someone who can teach them those things. Provide time for students to teach one another.

- **Baking blind:** have students work in pairs to make a simple meal, e.g. pikelets or a cordial drink. Blindfold one partner and ask the other person to help them cook.

- **Class discussion:** discuss and record how different people have strengths in different areas and how we need others help sometimes if we have difficulty managing in a particular area.

- **Class poster:** students are issued with two cards, one with the title *It is great that people have different strengths because ...* and the other titled *It is good to get help from others when ...* Students complete the sentences with one idea and attach to a class poster.

LESSON 3

Purpose : To share an understanding of ADHD and establish a climate of support to enable successful implementation of peer-assisted programmes.

Format

- Review and discuss concepts in last two lessons.

- **Post box:** place four pieces of paper with the following headings around the room and a cardboard box under each:
    - What is good about having friends?
    - What is it like to have no friends?
    - How do people who are lonely act?
    - How do you demonstrate friendship?

  Ask students to move around the room and write and post their ideas to each question. Discuss what has been recorded.

- Ask the target student to do an errand at this point if you think it best, or actively involve them in explaining the concept of ADHD.

- Explain that ADHD is a condition some people have which sometimes makes it hard for them to pay attention, be organised, behave sensibly and make friends.

- Discuss the fact that the target student has ADHD and what his/ her day must be like at school. Discuss ways the class thinks they could assist the student to manage better at school.

- Introduce the concept of the study buddy programme discussed in the work completion section of this book.

- If relevant introduce the **Circle of Friends** programme. The purpose is to foster a feeling of acceptance among peers and develop a circle of support around the student that may result in genuine friendships.

- Discuss class rewards for involvement, e.g. social rewards, personal growth, and a class game fortnightly. Ask students if they would like to volunteer to help the student and record names of those interested.

- **Chocolate race:** a relay game to conclude this series of lessons in which teams of six students take turns to try and consume a chocolate bar using a plastic knife and fork. Once a student has had a bite they run back to the next student who takes their turn with the knife and fork.

LESSON 4

Purpose : To provide training to peers who have volunteered that will equip them with the skills and knowledge to participate in the study buddy programme and circle of friends.

Format

- Implement the study buddy programme as previously outlined.

- Establish circle of friends by explaining the requirements of the programme, choosing who will do each day, issuing the associated sheet and deciding on where sheets will be returned to each day.

- Introduce and explain the study buddy programme to the target student. It is not necessary for the target student to be aware that the circle of friends programme is being implemented.

Circle of Friends

Name _____ **Day** _____

On the day shown try and do each of these things for your secret friend. After you have done each thing, colour in the box beside it. At the end of the day give the complete form to your teacher. You are a great person who cares about others. Thank you!

☐ say something kind to the person.

☐ have a conversation with the person.

☐ share or lend something to the person.

☐ ask the person to work with you.

☐ ask the person to join you in the playground.

94

Social Behaviour Goals GOAL

Student's name _____ **Teacher's name** _____

By signing this you agree to the goal set and will make an opportunity to achieve it.

Student's signature _____ **Teacher's signature** _____

Goal : _____

To achieve this goal I will _____

I will know it is achieved when _____

I expect to achieve it by this date _____

Self-assessment of how well I achieved my goal:

Goal : _____

I did / did not achieve my goal because I _____

_____

Teacher assessment

Other achievements I am proud of

Guided Playground Observation

Date _____ Area _____ Start time _____ Finish time _____

What social skill are you observing in the playground?	How did people show this social skill?	Do you have any comments?

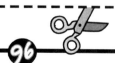

Playground Plan

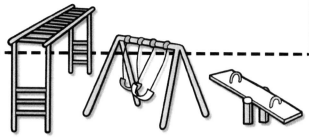

Name _____ Room _____

In the playground this student is expected to _____

_____

_____

_____

If this student does not meet these expectations this is what will happen _____

_____

_____

If this student does meet these expectations this is what will happen _____

_____

_____

	Monday	Tuesday	Wednesday	Thursday	Friday
Activity					
Play Mates					
Duty teacher signature					
Class teacher signature					

10 Teacher Intervention Plan

Target Student's name _____ Date implemented _____

Rules / expectations	Goals	Incentives / consequences

Strategies to manage behaviours	Strategies to assist with teacher directed instructions	Strategies to assist with work completion

Strategies to assist with organisation	Adaptations to classroom environment	Adaptations to presenting learning

Strategies to assist peer relationships	Strategies for parent collaboration	Strategies to assist with teacher relationship

Enlarge to A3 on photocopier and record the interventions you have decided to implement.